Writing Unbound

THOMAS NEWKIRK

Writing Unbound

**How
Fiction
Transforms
Student
Writers**

HEINEMANN
Portsmouth, NH

Heinemann
361 Hanover Street
Portsmouth, NH 03801–3912
www.heinemann.com

Offices and agents throughout the world

The author and publisher wish to thank those who have generously given permission to reprint borrowed material:

Figure 6–1: Image of Thomas R. Newkirk, swimming. Copyright © 2020 by University of New Hampshire. Reprinted with permission.

Acknowledgments for borrowed material continue on p. 150.

Library of Congress Cataloging-in-Publication Data
Names: Newkirk, Thomas, author.
Title: Writing unbound : how fiction transforms student writers / Thomas Newkirk.
Description: Portsmouth, NH : Heinemann, [2021] | Includes bibliographical references. | Identifiers: LCCN 2020050248 | ISBN 9780325092157
Subjects: LCSH: English language—Composition and exercises—Study and teaching (Middle School) | English language—Composition and exercises—Study and teaching (Secondary) | Fiction—Authorship—Study and teaching (Middle School) | Fiction—Authorship—Study and teaching (Secondary)
Classification: LCC LB1631 .N3785 2021 | DDC 428.0071/2—dc23
LC record available at https://lccn.loc.gov/2020050248

Editor: Margaret LaRaia and Heather Anderson
Production: Vicki Kasabian
Cover and text designs: Suzanne Heiser
Cover photo: © Shutterstock / koya979
Interior photos: © Houlton Archive / Getty Images (*F. Scott Fitzgerald*);
    © Photodisc / Getty Images / HIP (*clock*); © Shutterstock / intueri (*guitar tattoo*)
Typesetting: Kim Arney
Manufacturing: Valerie Cooper

Printed in the United States of America on acid-free paper
1 2 3 4 5   RWP   26 25 24 23 22 21
February 2021 Printing

To Peter Elbow,
mentor and friend

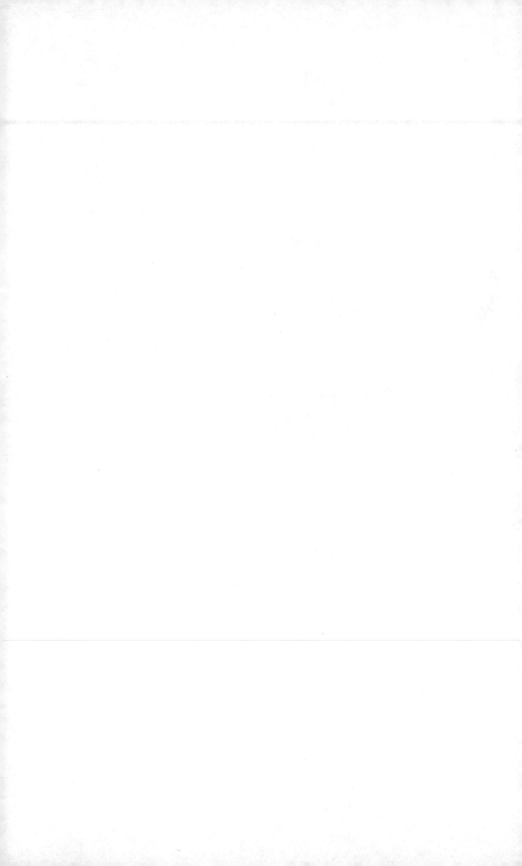

CONTENTS

ACKNOWLEDGMENTS

In *A Streetcar Named Desire*, Blanche DuBois admits that she has always depended on "the kindness of strangers." That is surely the case with this book. It is built on a set of interviews with student writers, all of them total strangers to me. They and their parents agreed to meet me in local libraries or through Zoom meetings to describe what fiction meant to them. They were my guides, my teachers, the beating heart of this book. I'll be forever grateful.

I want to thank several teachers who helped me locate these student guides. Tomasen Carey helped me contact students who participated in the University of New Hampshire's Writers Academy. She was also an invaluable early reader of a draft of this book. Laura Bradley put me in contact with several of her student novel writers. Thanks also to Marty Brandt, Kate McKenny, David Rockower, and Liz Gonzalez who helped me find writers.

Thanks to the corps of teachers, whom I also interviewed. These conversations gave me faith that writing was unbound and flourishing in classrooms across the country. Kathy Rowlands was instrumental in making many of these connections—so thanks to her for this, and for our long personal and professional friendship.

As an emeritus faculty member, I was able to get guidance on research procedures from Julie Simpson and Melissa McGee at Research Integrity Services at the University of New Hampshire. They suggested I use Zoom to do interviews—hard to imagine but I had never heard of Zoom. They showed me ways of securely storing data in Box, also new to me, and they helped me craft consent forms.

As I interviewed and wrote this book, I benefited from other qualitative researchers who occupy a permanent space in my consciousness and set the standards for this kind of work. The list is long—but always there are Shirley Brice Heath, Peter Johnston, Vivian Paley, Mike Rose, Anne Haas Dyson, Douglas Barnes, and Alfred Tatum. The book directly builds on the work of Jeff Wilhelm and Michael Smith, specifically *Reading Unbound*. With their permission I have borrowed from their title and their lines of questioning.

Since 1984, I have had the good fortune to work with Heinemann and cherish the support they have given me. It has been the perfect blend of high-level professionalism and close personal collaboration. So, thanks to the great team that saw this book through—Krysten Lebel, Kim Cahill, Suzanne Heiser, Sarah Fournier, Roderick Spelman, and Heather Anderson. Thanks also to Anne, my semi-anonymous copy editor, for her care in finding inconsistencies and omissions in the manuscript. Vicki Kasabian also gave it a very close reading, reviewed formatting, and oversaw details throughout the editing and production processes.

Margaret LaRaia was the main editor for this book, as she has been for three others I have written. I so appreciated her ability to get on my wavelength and urge me on. She helped me to stay true to the possibilities of the book, to be *unbound*.

Thanks, as always, to my wife, Beth, who listened to so much oral composing of this book that I suspect she is relieved to see it in print. She has been a constant source of support.

1

Writing Unbound

The Missed Opportunity of Fiction Writing

Bastian: How many wishes do I get?

Empress Moonchild: As many as you want. And the more wishes you make, the more magnificent Fantasia will become.

—From *The NeverEnding Story* (1984)

In the summer of 2004, my wife and I attended a Boston Red Sox game, where some filming for the movie *Fever Pitch* was being done. After the singing of the national anthem, the door of the Green Monster—a thirty-five-foot wall and scoreboard in left field—opened, and a man with a Sox shirt and chinos began a slow, labored walk toward the pitcher's mound.

It was Stephen King, the limp caused by a horrific 1999 accident in which he was hit in the breakdown lane—the other driver was travelling, as he often did, in the wrong lane. King remarked that it was as if one of his own demented characters came to life to injure him.

As he walked the three hundred feet to the mound, the crowd rose and applauded him. Soon we were all on our feet in sustained appreciation. I wondered if any other author could receive such a tribute from this crowd. (J. K. Rowling was the only name I could come up with.) Even if those standing had not read *Christine* or *The Shining* or other novels he has produced in his amazing career, they had seen movies and TV series; they may have been aware his stories were the basis for two superb movies, *The Shawshank Redemption* and *Stand by Me*. We may have been cheering his recovery from the accident, and perhaps his legendary generosity in his home state of Maine. Maybe all of that.

Whatever the reason, we knew that here was a man who had created a thrilling vision of horror. Like Rowling he has created a world, a kingdom. I once had a student who claimed that we love horror because it makes us feel fully present—nothing exists outside that moment of terror. We feel fully alive in our bodies—it affects our mind, heart, breathing, and skin. King takes us there. He writes for us.

And for the record, he threw a strike.

While King is a model for a virtual army of young and not-so-young writers, his brand of fiction has little place in the high school English reading curriculum—and no place, that I can see, in the writing curriculum. In fact, fiction writing disappears from our educational system around middle school, if it survives that long. The Common Core standards generally ignore it, along with narrative in general, in the upper grades. At this stage, writing is colonized, controlled, by the literature curriculum, and the focus often contracts to the analysis of literature. Mercifully, there are exceptions—the multigenre paper, and the elective creative writing course, which is often the first course to be cut in a crunch. But the fiction writing that does happen is usually off the formal educational grid.

And this off-grid writing is plentiful. The main FanFiction website contains 817,000 pieces written off the Harry Potter books, and 220,000 off the Twilight series. Over a million fictional pieces from those two series! Percy Jackson spinoffs are near the top of the list (72K) as are those built off *The Hunger Games* (45K) and *The Lord of the Rings* (55K). There are even submissions using the Bible (4.1K) and *Pride and Prejudice* (4.9K) and this is just for books. Two popular TV shows, *Glee* and *Supernatural*, both have more than 100,000 entries. Video games also spawn fiction with over 82K for *Pokémon* and 73K for *Kingdom Hearts*. More recently created sites, Quotev, Wattpad, and Archive of Our Own, have similarly huge numbers, and attract writers from across the globe. We can predict an exponentially greater number of unposted stories created by loyal followers.

Even in those schools that employ writing workshop approaches, fiction writing is marginalized or avoided, with memoir or personal narrative and, later on, the informational report or argument holding center stage.[1] Often this personal nonfiction is perceived as more authentic than fiction—especially high fantasy, which is seen as derivative. In college a student normally has to take at least up to three preliminary nonfiction writing courses before being allowed to elect a fiction writing course, assuming one is available. And even then it is unlikely that they would be able to attempt popular forms like the graphic novel.

All of which leads to a question that has puzzled me my entire career. If reading fiction is beneficial, if, as some research indicates, it builds empathy, reading stamina, vocabulary, and cultural knowledge, if it provides entry into appealing vicarious worlds (e.g., Chiaet 2013)—why can't the same be said for writing fiction? Am I missing something here? Jeff Wilhelm (1997) has shown that readers need to "be the book" to feel present in the book—and writers can also "be the book," as in the case of one young student I interviewed who created JoJo, the junk food ant, a recurring character in his stories:

> **Mike:** Sometimes I feel like I'll write about this little ant named JoJo—a junk food ant—and he goes on these little adventures and usually gets hurt. So sometimes when I write about him, I make him like talking. I feel like I'm him, like when the Red Sox hit a grand slam and he gets caught on the ball, I feel like I'm flying through space like this (*he leans back in his chair and mimes holding on to the baseball*).
>
> **TN:** So when you're writing you feel like you are in the air?
>
> **Mike:** Yeah, when he gets hurt in the air, and I'm kind of like up there. I'm JoJo. (Newkirk 2002, 67)

---

1 In this book I make the claim that opportunities for writing fiction diminish as students move upward in the secondary grades. This view was confirmed by the teachers I interviewed, and it fits my own observations. Unfortunately, I have not been able to locate any recent, comprehensive surveys of the kinds of writing required in middle and high school. The 2011 NAEP Writing Assessment (using data from 2007) does show a shift in the high school years from writing "to convey experience" to writing that explains and argues. The NAEP Reading Assessment similarly shows a shift to "essay" writing in the high school years—though "stories" (likely personal experience narratives) persist as a common assignment (summarized in Applebee and Langer [2009]).

David Coleman, a chief writer of the ELA Common Core standards, has famously stated that the most common types of writing in high school English classes are the reader response and the personal narrative—a focus he is highly critical of (2012). Applebee and Langer's own study of middle and high school writing instruction shows that students are rarely required to write at the length that fiction writers I interview attempt—and that the "essay" writing they do is often formulaic and often shaped by high-stakes test expectation (2011). In sum, I feel confident in my claim that opportunities for fiction writing in the high school ELA curriculum are seriously limited in most schools, except in special electives and writing for school literary magazines. Ultimately, readers will need to assess this claim against their own situations and experiences.

If we gain insight into the human character by reading fiction, why can't we get similar insight (or more profound insight) by creating characters? Even if our aim is still to make better fiction readers, won't writing fiction attune students to craft, structure, and detail as they learn to read like a writer? If we want to build a love of writing, why in the world would we want to rule out the option to write fiction, emulating the genres and cultural storytelling that is so deeply popular outside school walls? Why do schools so willingly accept these handicaps and limitations?

Here are some possibilities.

Obstacles and Resistance
Teachers Themselves Have Had Little Experience Writing Fiction

This is a variant of a bigger problem—that English teachers are rarely required to take writing courses as part of their preparation. At the University of New Hampshire, where I taught for thirty-seven years, the only required writing course for prospective teachers was first-year writing (and that was required of all students)—an example of the reading–writing imbalance. It is exceedingly rare that a prospective teacher would take the prerequisites that would enable them to register for a fiction-writing course. And it is, as I noted earlier, unlikely that they will be taught versions of fiction that their future students will want to write.

The Fiction Writing That Students Choose to Do Is Often Imitative of Low-Status Forms of Entertainment

Young writers are drawn to plot, to action, to writing versions of movies and video games that appear—to a certain sensibility—as less "authentic" than nonfiction genres like the memoir. Borrowing characters and plot elements (and weapons) from preexisting stories violates an expectation of originality and personal examination of experiences. (As if memoir is not, itself, a preexisting genre.) Popular youth genres, particularly those selected by boys, have traditionally been labeled "escapist."

One of the least attractive traits in adults is the inability—or unwillingness—to imagine literary gratifications that we don't feel (though we perhaps once did). And then to rationalize this inability, this limitation of imagination, as a claim that certain popular genres are incapable of eliciting thoughtful engagement. We fail to decenter, to take an inquiry stance, to learn why someone might enjoy a literary genre that we don't (or won't). Some genres of writing, we come to believe, are capable of eliciting complex responses, and some aren't—by their very nature.

This view has been powerfully challenged by a number of scholars, most notably Janice Radway in her sympathetic investigation of women reading romance novels (1984). My own approach is deeply indebted to the work of Jeffrey Wilhelm and Michael Smith—in fact my own title mirrors theirs, as does my argument. Wilhelm and Smith begin with a set of provocative questions:

> Might kids gravitate to the kinds of texts they need? Might they experience a deep fulfillment that we don't completely understand when they read those books? Might passionate readers of marginalized texts—those books that many parents and teachers disapprove of at some level—be choosing books that help them build on new interests, become competent in new ways, and grow beyond their current selves? (2014, 9)

Yes. Yes. Yes. They found that even genres we might dismiss as superficial and escapist—like vampire stories—could elicit profound reflections on sexual attraction. Texts do not set hard boundaries on what readers can do with them—a fact driven home to me when I listened to literacy expert James Gee spend a brilliant hour on an aspirin bottle label.

An argument for fiction writing can mirror the one Wilhelm and Smith make for the reading of marginalized genres. Young writers who devote themselves to seemingly endless postapocalyptic stories *are gaining something by it*—and to understand that gratification we need to ask them questions. We cannot presume to know their realities.

Inexperienced Writers Have Difficulty Managing Plots, Leading to Unplanned and Excessively Long Stories

True. True. True. But there are ways, including storyboarding, that can help with planning. In addition, there are very popular short forms like flash fiction that can be introduced.

Yet I would like to make the case for this long writing. When I speak with the really fluent and accomplished writers who have taken my first-year writing course, many of them could look back to a time when they wrote at length—maybe a journal they kept up, or a long novel they wrote with a friend, chapter after chapter. Unlike many of their peers, who panicked about meeting a page requirement, these writers had an expansive sense of what writing could be—they had *felt* that openness, that the blank page (or screen) was an invitation and not a threat. That writing could unfold. They have trouble staying within the page limit—a good problem in my view.

I realize that it may seem like I am supporting overwriting, *and I am.* Almost all the good young writers push description and dialogue and plot to the limit, often boring to any outside reader. It's the same with athletes— watch promising middle school athletes. They will often charge into a hopeless layup, dive for a ball clearly out of reach, attempt the impossible pass. Often their bodies are not under full control. Their game is excessive. Yet that daring, that excess, that lack of caution, is a virtue. Good coaches know that. Control will come later. In the same way, the overwriter can be taught to control the gift of excess, but the underwriter has no awareness that this excess is even a possibility.

But even this inevitable difficulty can be helped by instruction and planning tools, as we will see in the interviews with skilled teachers. Concepts like *plot beats*, drawn from screenwriting, can be attractive supports. When students have difficulties inherent in a task, the solution is not to avoid the task, particularly one as appealing as fiction writing. The proper response is to offer support—and we will meet teachers up to that challenge.

Concern About Violence and Other Themes Students Write About

When I was conducting research on young boys writing I had to confront a puzzling double standard. In many schools, there was a "no violence" policy for writing. No fights, killing, stabbing, plane crashes. In one school there was an absurd rule that no character in a fictional piece could do something that wasn't allowed in the school. When I visited schools with such restrictions, I asked, "Does the same rule apply to reading?"

There would be a pause. And then the inevitable, "Well, no." Of course, "no." Without violence, or the threat of violence (physical, psychological), there would be no plots. No literature at all. No Bible. No *Hamlet*. No *BFG*. No *Beowulf* with its tremendous description of Beowulf breaking his sword in Grendel's eye. It was as if literature, with all its violence, was uplifting and humanizing—but a student writing on these themes might need a visit to the guidance counselor. It seemed to me this was just one more example of

Deborah Brandt's (2015) claim, that reading and writing have hardly been viewed as parallel systems—writing is somehow more dangerous and in need of suppression.

I wondered if this double standard was not also an inadvertent acknowledgment of the power of writing for the writer, of a deeper and more dangerous engagement that occurs when a writer takes on the same dark themes that animate great literature. To put it yet another way: to read about deviance is a benign experience, yet to inhabit the mind of the deviant or *invent* scenes in which violence occurs exposes a troubling morbidity.

The writer must dwell longer, must work out the visual picture, must create—and it may be that the deeper identification with the violence is what alarms adults. It may seem to reveal a dangerous attraction to violence, an unhealthy obsession, even an unethical acceptance of the inevitability of violence. Yet this danger can be attractive, and hardly a sign of psychological danger. Smith and Wilhelm claim that horror stories provide a "psychological container for examining fears and shadow contents" (2014, 143), a claim that makes sense for writing as well as reading.

Fiction writing allows for a greater psychological range than do most nonfiction forms. The writer can imagine extremes of fear, anger, resentment, and, yes, evil that they don't and wouldn't want to experience in real life. By contrast, the personal essays that students write—for example, stories of growth and surmounting challenges in college application essays—typically operate in a more tightly defined moral or psychological range (Vidali 2007; Wight 2017). Claims for the "authenticity" of the personal essay ignore the guardrails that shape disclosure, often in a safely moralistic way.

Making a place for fiction writing in middle and high schools entails challenges. Teachers are often given (or give themselves) the impossible task of determining if a "dark" story is a precursor to violence or self-harm. Or even that it might be a cause. For some reason this is not a problem with reading. Fiction writing also poses issues concerning limits, appropriate language, sexism, stereotyping, and placing other students in uncomfortable positions. Students will test limits.

True. But in my work with boys and literacy I became convinced that these issues can be talked about: the very genres they want to write impose limits. Plots must unfold, and not simply be just a train wreck of action. Characters must interest the reader and act, even when being deviant, in a plausible way. Violence has its place, but it often works best when something is left to the imagination—and I am convinced that it is not violence but suspense and anticipation (and fear) that is the characteristic writers would want to achieve if they could.

We need to get beyond a crude "if-you-write-it-you-want-to-do-it" mentality that can censor student writing. Whether we like it or not, we are attracted to deviance, danger, catastrophe, so long as we can experience them at a safe distance. It doesn't mean we, or our students, are warped or deviant. If we see a slowdown for an auto accident, the moral side of our brain hopes that it is a minor fender bender—but there is a side of us that is excited and gratified by a major smashup. To deny that attraction is an act of bad faith.

Lack of Fit with Standards That Focus on Being "College and Career Ready"

On the surface, the very thin surface, this priority makes sense. Few students will go on to be conventionally published novel writers, though they will need to write reports, résumés, letters, evaluations. Therefore it makes sense for the "grand shift" around sixth grade to the more functional types of writing—to be, as the expression goes, "college and career ready."

I call this bias, the *cattle-chute vision of preparation*. If you want someone to end up at point A, you need a narrow and direct pathway to A. All student writing needs to be—so to speak—Type A. To write Type B or C or D is to deviate from the most efficient and direct pathway, to waste time and dissipate effort. This is why a creative writing elective is often viewed as a kind of indulgence, unrelated to the main mission of high school writing. I think of the advice that the young Dav Pilkey received: that he would never make a living drawing silly cartoons about a principal who thinks he is Captain Underpants. That, of course, was several million book sales ago.

The cattle-chute mentality misses the point that (1) there are goals for writing that are not purely pragmatic and career oriented (like poetry writing—virtually ignored in the Common Core standards); and (2) even if we take this extremely pragmatic view, skills can migrate from type to type. Fiction writing entails reflection, analysis, close observation, internal debate—all broadly useful skills that can feed other kinds of writing, even the scientific report. To create characters in conflict, the writer must imagine opposing points of view—a skill needed in argumentation. Fiction writers are typically excellent reviewers, essayists, and nonfiction writers. They don't fall apart when they move outside of fiction—they excel.

The cattle-chute model also misrepresents narrative as a singular type of writing, often part of the triad, narrative/informational/argument. Yet we have abundant evidence from the field of cognition that narrative is not a discrete type of writing—it is our primary mode of understanding, and it underlies all writing (Newkirk 2014). Grant Faulkner, the executive director of NaNoWriMo (the National Novel Writing Month organization, which has brought November novel writing to ten thousand classrooms nationwide), makes the case this way:

> We are meaning-making creatures, and the way we make meaning in the world is through our stories. I happen to believe that all nonfiction has storytelling elements. I fear that that is going to be lost. I think that kids can be more attuned to the storytelling elements that go into nonfiction by doing it directly, through fiction writing. (personal interview)

This storytelling, in his view, is directly applicable to other types of writing "because if you look at any academic paper, any research paper, it has a narrative arc. It has points of narrative tension, it has characters. It's a story in the end."

He added that any student who manages to write a thirty- or forty-thousand-word novel in a month will hardly be intimidated by any future writing assignment.

Fiction writing can also offer an experience that I feel is crucial to enjoying writing: the feeling that writing generates writing—that a word suggests the next word or phrase, that we can listen to writing and sense what it suggests. A verb invites an object; a noun a clarifying clause. A conflict invites dialogue, action invites reflection, a difficulty that a character faces invites planning. A plot unfolds. This is what fluency feels like, looks like. The great dividing line between writers and nonwriters is the capacity to enter this receptive state, to feel and respond to these invitations. As Montaigne wrote centuries ago, he could keep on writing "as long as there was ink and paper in the world."

Fiction writing is not the only avenue for this development of fluency—journals, day books, and other low-threshold writing can do the trick—but writing lengthy stories is ideal for this purpose. Even for young writers, there can always be a sequel, characters who never die.

Time. Time. Time

When I was a graduate student in Texas during the 1970s, I recall the legislature passing a new requirement that students should be taught fire prevention. Who could argue against that? But the question was: Which subject-area teachers should teach this required unit?

It was decided that since it would involve reading and writing, the best place for it would be in the English classroom. This was one maybe outlandish example of a chronic problem, the proliferation of expectations, standards, competencies—to the point where English Language Arts (ELA) teachers are haunted by the feeling that they can't do anything thoroughly or well. While it has been argued for decades that writing should take place "across the curriculum," the major, sometimes exclusive, responsibility ends up on our shoulders. And even for teachers committed to fiction writing, it's a tough fit in the curriculum. Stories take time and are often far longer than more contained forms of writing—an editorial, for example, which can be held to a few paragraphs.

Still, there are things we can do to create space for writing, including fiction writing—things under our control. The great Shaker song has the repeating line, "it's a gift to be simple." It's also hard work—the spare lines of Shaker furniture, the appealing lack of adornment, take exquisite skill to perfect. Looking at the clutter, the crowding, of the ELA curriculum, I'd like to propose two ways of opening up space for writing, including fiction writing.

Don't Let Writing-Like Activities Substitute for Writing

In my day it was grammar instruction that crowded out writing. Now, it might be a spelling program, or a vocabulary program—complete with worksheets, exercises, quizzes. These "peripherals" make money for publishers, they conform well to objective grading. They fill the grade book, and they may have some marginal benefit to learning to write. But we need to fight to make writing (and not writing-like activities) the center of our work, we need to learn to say no and teach these features of writing in context.

Don't Talk So Much

Sorry to be so rude. But deep in our DNA there must be some image of teaching where we are talking—instructing, giving directions, up front. Just walk past about any class. Studies of teacher lessons affirm that there is a deeply ingrained recitation script where the teacher takes two out of every three turns (Mehan 1979). Teacher asks question–student answers–teacher responds to answer. But if we see writing (and reading) as studio subjects, similar to art class, the time focus is on producing—with the teacher commenting, encouraging.

Often when I share research interest with my university colleagues, I feel like a total fraud. One of the faculty members I swim with is doing work on subatomic particles—quarks, antiquarks, gluons, hadrons—with non-integer multiples of electric charges. And all I was doing was saying, "Keep it simple." We don't need all this stuff. I felt like the frustrated coach in *Bull Durham*, "This is a simple game—ya throw the ball, ya hit the ball, ya catch the ball."

There are to be sure other major barriers, including the time to read, respond, and grade, that will be addressed later. It's not really simple—neither is baseball.

Bad Fiction

I was speaking to a very gifted writing teacher whose students *did* have the chance to write fiction. He was discussing some of the challenges he faced, and he paused, looked me in the eye, and said, "I'll be truthful, Tom, it pains me to read bad fiction. And that's what most students write."

It was my turn to pause, a bit surprised, and I asked him, "Don't all beginning writers write badly in some way? Is there something about 'bad fiction writing' that makes it more painful to read than a bad argument?" We both puzzled about this. It may be that we are so used to reading fiction—but not arguments—for a kind of literary pleasure, that we are bothered when we don't get it, or when we only get it in momentary flashes. Even a rudimentary, predictable argument can be functional: in fact, we get them all the time on cable news. But—and I'm speculating—amateur fiction can be a more irritating form of shortfall.

If that is the case, this "irritability" can get in the way of effective teaching. It can make us less forgiving of the approximations and imitations of beginning writers. I remember reading W. Jackson Bates' biography of John Keats (1963), and I was struck by how bad his early poetry was. This bias can close us off from the sense of achievement (and pleasure) that the writers take in their own work and cause us to miss those flashes of skill.

· ·

A confession. I am not the ideal person to explore adolescent fiction writing. In fact, for years I shared the prejudices and reluctances that I have identified. To put it more bluntly I was a literary snob, priding myself on reading "good literature" and being able to distinguish it from beach books and other "trash." I winced at reading the long fictional stories students wrote and agreed with many of my colleagues that students just wrote "bad fiction." I was never a fiction writer myself, in school or after. I never immersed myself in fandom, never devoted myself that way, not even during the Harry Potter phenomenon. I would flunk any quiz on popular culture.

I am writing this book as an outsider—which, after all, is not a bad starting point, to begin in acknowledged ignorance. But I needed insiders, tour guides, to point the way—to explain the sources of their fiction writing, to describe the gratifications of this work. So I located young writers and writing teachers willing to talk to me. In some cases these writers attended the summer Writers Academy in Durham, New Hampshire. Others were recommended to me by teachers I had worked with. These students, let me emphasize, are *not* representative of all students; they are a subculture in schools, often feeling somewhat alone in their passion. But I believe that, as they make their case for fiction writing in this book, readers will sense the missed opportunity in schools where writing is tightly controlled. My interviewees had a lot to say about that!

These writers sent me samples of their fiction, in some cases whole novels, which I read before interviewing them, some in-person at school and public libraries, others through the miracle of Zoom. In all I conducted approximately forty student interviews and fifteen teacher interviews, which form the core of this book. The student interviews vary in length from twenty to fifty-eight minutes, and they are built around several questions or invitations that were consistent:

1. Tell me about your history as a fiction reader or writer.

2. What is the attraction of fiction?

3. How is writing fiction different for you than nonfiction?

4. If you were to take me inside your head while writing fiction, what would I see?

5. Do you have the opportunity to write fiction in school? If not, why do you think that is?

6. What is the best help you received from a teacher about writing fiction?

7. Do you have readers? What do you find helpful in their response?

8. What advice would you give to students who want to write fiction?

9. What advice would you give to teachers to be good teachers of fiction writing?

I also posed questions related to the particular piece of fiction they shared with me. As much as possible, I wanted the feeling of an author interview that you might hear on public radio.

In my interviews with teachers, I was interested in the place of fiction writing in their schools, particularly how they justified it, how they framed assignments, their role as reader and evaluator. I was interested in how they managed plot and length, which to me would be mind-boggling when students wrote novels, as they did in one classroom.

I listened to the interviews multiple times, noting recurring themes or similar points that students and teachers brought up. Like any qualitative researcher I was looking for patterns. For example, I found that students often spontaneously brought up their dislike of the ways in which rubrics are used, and I began to pay special attention to the reasons why. I try to bring in these comments using a "theme and variation" method, showing multiple instances of student comment on a topic. This is, in a way, a check against highlighting the interesting but outlier response of a single student. I also tried to link individual students' comments to their own fictional work. As an example, I came to see the deep pleasure many of them had in depicting "action" and I would make note of where they did that in their writing. I came to deeply appreciate my tour guides in this project, and I hope that I do justice to their insights and creative work.

. . . .

One day during my high school years, say 1962, I was home sick, and my dad passed on to me a Signet paperback with a picture of a young man wearing an odd red hat and with a similarly odd title, *The Catcher in the Rye*. I'd never heard of the book. I recall reading aloud the opening and coming to "all that David Copperfield kind of crap," thinking this is a book written for me, in my language—the first time I ever felt that way.

Now, of course, the book is standard school reading, rarely challenged anymore, and I suppose students are writing the same "essays" about it that Salinger mocks in the novel. All of which raises the question of what happens when any art form or media becomes part of school. Does it lose its edge, become domesticated? Is it converted into a moral tract with "themes"? Is rap in the classroom really rap?

This is a question for fiction writing—does it lose its edge, the personal ownership and freedom that writers feel as they compose for no grade, no teacher? While I recognize that this is a danger, the history of the English curriculum deals with the shifting boundary between the popular and the academic. Anne Gere (1994) has written extensively of the "extra-curriculum"—informal reading and writing groups—that have progressively become part of the curriculum (for a long time American literature was not taught—and up until the 1960s it couldn't count for the major at my own university!). Women's studies, film studies, courses in graphic novel, multi-modal composing, even creative writing—all began outside the established curricular grid. Schools and universities gradually—and sometimes grudgingly—brought them in, to maintain relevancy and attract students.

It simply makes no sense to deny students the opportunity to write in the genres they choose to read. Why in the world should we undermine our efforts to engage students with writing? If reading fiction is humanizing and valuable—the same (and perhaps a stronger) case can be made for writing.

Enough. Time to dive in.

2

Meet Ernest

> Some people don't get the "What if?" Some people
> like the easier what ifs of what if this happened to
> so-and-so, in modern day. Other people can't stand
> that kind of stuff and that is what fantasy is for.
>
> —Helen, quoted in *Reading Unbounded*

We'll start by spending some time with Ernest, who has been an avid fiction writer since second grade. I will leave it to him to open up the major themes of this book. Consider this short chapter a kind of overture, an introduction to the themes we will explore in more depth later.

Before meeting Ernest, who was beginning ninth grade in a local high school, I had a chance to read a chapter from the novel he was working on, accompanied by a list of possible characters—100 of them on an Excel spreadsheet—for his planned novel, *The Hundred*, an exponentially large expansion of *The Hunger Games* plot. For each character there was a column for status (alive/dead), injuries, partnerships, enemies, importance (main/side character), role, age, sex, and kills. Simply generating the 100 names seemed to me a task, and some of the names were promising: Gretchen Mallace, Sweet Gravy, Jake Dorkly, and my personal favorite, Happy Grimm.

Like many of his fiction-writing peers, Ernest was interested in big what-ifs—and attracted to postapocalyptic worlds where the social order had been destroyed and he could remake it. The slate was wiped clean. As Ernest explained to me, he likes to place his stories at least 100 years into the future so that he can design his own worlds with no obligation for a realistic portrayal of contemporary life. Here he sets the scene in his novel *The Test* in his first chapter, "Ana":

> There I stood. Looking over a rocky cliff into the refreshing lake.
> I was so high up I couldn't see my reflection in the clear water.
> The silence was cut off by metallic vacuum in the distance,
> keeping the air clean so it wouldn't kill us.

She meets her friend Shayne, who retains a "New Yorkish accent," unusual because "only a few factions still maintain any form of unique speech. . . ." Ana and Shayne are concerned about a "Picking" that seems imminent (clear echoes of *The Hunger Games* and distant ones of "The Lottery"). Ernest has us almost immediately in a polluted, post-disaster world where air has to be treated and water must be purified and is rationed by a government that we are already suspicious of. (Ernest notes that because of this pollution, few people know how to swim.) The air is so bad that Ana must throw up once a day, sometimes twice, with some blood. Ernest's description of the government officials in PanGaea, the ones orchestrating the Picking, is eerie:

> The government officials spoke into the mike like they were
> afraid they might catch poverty if they spoke too close and had
> prosthetics that made them constantly smile.

Ana is chosen, the announcement coming from her own father, a council member. Ana's reaction:

> My whole world went silent. I could hear every breath, every
> drop of sweat, every thought. My heart stopped beating. Is this
> what everyone went through?

The stage is set for his up to 100 characters.

For a half hour, in the conference room of a quaint local library, Ernest would be one of my first tour guides. And since his story of engagement anticipates so many others I heard, we'll spend some time with Ernest.

For Ernest, it all started in second grade with a story called "Cosmos":

> It was a sci-fi story about these three genius schoolkids
> who were abducted by aliens, and they had to fight some
> intergalactic space threat.

That led to "Son of the Wild":

> Which was inspired by my favorite author, Rick Riordan,
> and his whole Percy Jackson series. It was about Peter
> Woodland, who was the son of Pan, who lived in New York.
> But after his dad was killed in an explosion he stowed
> away to St. Martin, where he lived the rest of his life until
> adventure brought him back to America where he had to
> fight a giant snake, basically.

Which led to "The Boy Who Lived on the Bear":

> . . . which is about these giant creatures invading Earth, or
> they're already on Earth but invading the land. And then this
> boy got adopted by one of them, which was a bear. And then
> he builds a home and lived on it, and then he has to fight the
> titan army.

Which led to his current mega-project, a dystopian novel, *The Test*, which I have already quoted. In many of these stories and projected video games there are recurring characters—Theron Black and Kyle Lavender—that have been a part of his storytelling for years.

Like many other students I interviewed, Ernest had a partner, James, who wrote with him.

> He and I have a very similar psychology when it comes to
> creating. We have had similar ideas for video games, for
> books. Like recently he came up with this awesome idea of
> people who had special powers based on the periodic table
> elements, and that reminded me that a couple of years ago I
> made a book about—it wasn't the periodic table elements—it
> was different elements like fire, water, earth. We just come
> up with these amazing universes and I think that's the bond
> of our friendship.

One of their most complex joint efforts involves creating a video game, *Steve*. His description went on for several minutes, but here is the gist of it:

> There was this kid named Steve who was a technological genius who started making robots to help people, and he made this company called Steve. But he didn't think anyone would take him seriously, so he hired this older guy to pretend to be him. And basically, at first they started inventing like metal arms to help people who . . . help amputees, people . . . metallic lungs to help people with lung cancer or whatever, basically metallic organs to help people whose organs didn't work anymore.
>
> And then eventually World War III started, and he started building weapons out of all this technology. And then when he won World War III for America, that's when he started going a bit crazy. And then he took over America and he took over the world. No one could stop him because almost everyone had at least one Steve robotic part in them, so he could just shut down that robotic part and they would die. So they had to follow him.

It only gets more complicated.

Much of this collaboration with James took place on the bus to and from school. As Ernest explains it, they have very different styles of composing that complement each other. They are currently working on a TV show (eight seasons, twenty episodes per season!):

> When it comes to producing ideas, I'm like a Gatling gun and he's like a sniper. I'm like constantly shooting out ideas and not all of them land and get into the show. Most of them I forget about or James denies them. James is like a sniper rifle because he doesn't shoot as often but when he does it almost always makes it in. It's almost always a good idea.

This is a good example of what Ann Haas Dyson (1996) calls "the social work" of literacy. Clearly the collaboration helps in the creation of these epic stories. But this process of composing fosters and sustains the friendship.

Another form of social work occurs in the stories themselves, often in the dialogue. Characters play out their relationships, sometimes joking, teasing, challenging—enacting friendships. We see this in the exchanges between Ana and Shayne as they contemplate their situation before the Picking. Shayne tells her she has nothing to worry about, kissing her on the cheek. She asks why she shouldn't worry. He leans in, his mouth right up to her ear:

> "Cause you're a nobody," he whispered.
>   "Shut up peasant boy," I lightly brushed him back.
>   "Fair enough, fair enough." He laughed. "You really don't have to worry. Peasants can't be picked."
>   "Okay, that's enough." His face was getting red.

Shayne is carrying a wicker basket that Ana is curious about.

> We came to a small drop off that led straight down to clear water, "I'll give it to you, but it will cost you." He said, doing his best to impersonate an epic narrator (Which wasn't very good).

Ernest uses this kind of interplay to develop the teasing relationship of his two main characters, who are clearly attracted to each other.

Mr. Julius Burn

I wanted Ernest to say something about his writing and characterization, so I invited him to pick a section from a story that we could talk about. He picked a story that he wrote in eighth into ninth grade, that featured his favorite and most complex character, Julius Burn. Simply to locate this excerpt in his novel is to risk becoming lost in the labyrinthine plots Ernest so enjoys.

The following exchange occurs early in the novel—Burn is in an unstimulating science class with an odd substitute teacher who seems to focus only on gasses and acts inappropriately with students, purposely showing "cleavage." At this point, she just appears to Burn as a bad teacher, but in reality she is part of a huge plot by the evil character Rudd to bring Burn and others onto the dark side (they are lulled into passivity by the gases). She is in reality a monster, as are the other "substitutes" that have replaced the regular teachers. This confrontation occurs after class when Burn has openly accused her of having an affair with the principal.

> "You can't prove that." She hissed.
>   "Actually . . ." I shuffled through my backpack and pulled out a tape. "I do have proof." She was too stunned to speak.
>   "Now, you can give me that detention slip which I know you

have waiting for me, but then this little tape might just get out." Most people would be scared to talk back to a teacher, but I had little to no respect for Mrs. Calvereto. She hardly knows science, only teaches us about gases, lowers her top for students who get bad grades for "Motivation," and worst of all, she's just a substitute. Last month, our old teacher left, and she took over. Just what happened to most teachers around the school.

"Young man." She growled. Uh oh. "You have the audacity to threaten me in my classroom?"

"Oh, this is your classroom? I thought this was a placeholder job."

I asked Ernest what he liked about this character.

I like him because he's kind of controversial. He's not necessarily a good person—he's kind of like Holden from *Catcher in the Rye*. He doesn't like people who are fake and think they're better than everyone else. But there's the whole discussion about being brave and being stupid. There has to be a point where you realize that doing this wouldn't be brave—it's just a bad time to do that. He's very charismatic but he's not very good at understanding social situations. Normally you'd think he has to grow up because he has to fight an invasion—but in the story he keeps this immature mentality. He thinks people are natural liars. He thinks the world doesn't deserve what's best for it.

Yet at the same time, in the dystopian world Ernest creates, this cynicism, while a handicap, is not unreasonable—because there is no clear line between good and bad. Even the superheroes in the story provoke a crisis that they resolve to show they are needed.

And Burn asks the question—what separates the hero from the villain? And his answer to that question is—nothing. The only thing that separates a hero and a villain is perspective—what side you're on. Which I think is very true. In *Star Wars*, the Empire thinks they're the good guys—the rebels are the villains. But we saw the movie from the perspective of the rebels—so the rebels are the heroes.

The Writing Process

As I listened to Ernest, it seemed his mind was literally swarming with plot ideas, and I asked about how they came to him:

> I heard this quote. I can't remember who said it, but, "You get your best ideas when you're bored or tired." And sometimes I'll get these amazing ideas just in my bed and I'll start writing them down. I'll typically get them . . . I do this thing; it's kind of embarrassing, but I just kind of run around my house while kind of gesticulating with my arms, just kind of being like, "This will happen in this scene, and that would happen." Kind of like acting it out minorly. And that's how I get most of my ideas. That's where I get most of my inspiration.

He noted that he also rehearsed his plots with his parents, until they were overwhelmed by the detail and sent him off to write.

Midway through the interview he mentioned that he has been diagnosed with ADHD and I wondered how that affected his fiction writing:

> I'm constantly thinking of different things even when I'm focusing on something else, so when I'm writing I'll be thinking of a different story. Academic-wise it can get in the way, but creative writing-wise it helps. Like, academic-wise it's hard for me to focus on what the teacher's trying to say. But creative-wise it helps me focus. It helps me constantly think of ideas. Even when it looks like I'm not doing anything, I am in my head.
>
> I sometimes have to play with the paranoia I have. The thing about creativity is that it's a blessing and a curse because you hear one thud downstairs and then you start thinking, "Is it a killer? Is it a demon? What is it?" And then that's something that I've always struggled with. But when it comes to creatively writing or thinking of a plot it helps because I can always think of different viewpoints.

Like many of the students I interviewed Ernest feels that school writing is controlled in a way he finds unappealing. The logic goes like this—all writing has to be evaluated, and in order to be evaluated it must have clear guidelines spelled out in rubrics. This evaluative structure was called a *filter* by another student I interviewed. The price of this "objectivity" and clarity is a loss of freedom, at least as Ernest sees it:

> My creative writing is a lot more restricted when they tell me what to do. And I'll admit, most of my creative writing gets done in school, but not when they tell me to. I'm just kind of writing in my own time. But I feel when they do ask me to do it it's a lot more constricted because they have guidelines. I like to make my stories a lot more extreme, like with some cuss words, some gore, because I like to make my stories realistic. But I obviously can't do that stuff when I'm writing for the school.

I asked him why he thought that was:

> I think it's just because they like order. They like things to go according to plan. And the thing about creativity is that it never goes according to plan. It has no order to it because creativity's this wonderful tool that I've been gifted with. I think the school doesn't really like that. I think they encourage you to be creative but creative in their way, not yours.
> The school wants you to do what they want you to do, and I can't really describe that. And maybe college is going to be different. I hope it is. But I think at least for public school systems it's more controlled and more kind of guidelined. There's a lot of rubrics and this kind of stuff that tells you this is what you can do and this is what you can't do.

In parallel fashion, Ernest finds the reading curriculum constraining and unappealing because of the lack of choice:

> I don't like being told what to read because I need freedom and independence when it comes to what I read and write. Like, *Lord of the Flies*, which we are reading now, is an interesting book, but I don't get it because I think the author is a bit too heavy-handed on symbolism—where he starts to ignore "what is" for "what it means." . . .
> Sometimes I'm glad I am told to pick up those books [he later mentions liking Sherman Alexie]. But most of the time I

think I could be reading something else. And then there's the whole "answer these questions about it"—because when I read I just want to get lost in the world that the author created, and when I have to answer questions it makes me feel like I can't get lost anymore.

Two observations. I think Ernest is exactly right about *Lord of the Flies*. And second, he seems to be advocating for the importance of the "reading zone" where "Everything around you disappears and all you care about are the characters" (Atwell and Merkel 2016, 24). That, clearly, is where Ernest wants to be when he reads fiction—and when he writes it.

One question that I had for all the writers I interviewed was Why? Why do it? Is it about reaching an audience? Or is the pleasure coming primarily in the act of writing itself? Is it a transaction with a reader—or it is it an advanced form of play with the gratification coming from the process of creation? While Ernest would talk about readers, and clearly had friends from the University of New Hampshire Writers Academy who read his work, it was the world-creating possibilities that he clearly loved:

I've always had this fear of not being able to control my own life. But when I'm writing my own book I do have control. I guess I'm kind of like the god of that series because I can choose if someone lives or dies, I can choose if someone's happy or sad.

I'm a middle child, so I don't have a lot of power in the house, because my brother can do whatever he wants and my little sister can do whatever she wants because she's the youngest. My brother's the oldest. He has the most independence. She has the most reliance on my parents. So I think writing these creative stories gives me a lot more power.

The attraction of fiction for Ernest is power to make a world, make a future, to be in control, as he (and others I interviewed) said, "I can be a sort of god."

I remember years ago I watched a first grader named Adam in a writing group conference. The world as he created it was under attack, in danger. And a girl raised her hand and asked him, "Will the world survive?"

Adam hesitated, and she asked again, "Adam, will the world survive?" Still he paused. "I'm thinking, I'm thinking."

It was all in his hands.

Don't Hold Back

At the end of our interview I asked Ernest the same question I asked all the writers I interviewed: "If you could give advice to young fiction writers, what would you say?" He paused, took a deep breath, and began by describing how he had led his life by how others would judge him. "I have passed on a lot of opportunities because I was worried how other people would judge me." As an example he described how he quit wearing hoodies to high school because of how his classmates would perceive him. Even with his writing he has been keenly aware of the judgment of others.

> So I guess my advice would be—don't do that. When it comes to writing—that is the place where judgment leaves the building. Look at Stephen King, one of the most famous and praised authors in the world. And his stories are questionable, like the ending of *It*. He has very questionable content but he's celebrated as an amazing author because he doesn't hold back. He doesn't think, *I wonder if the reader is going to think this is too far, too offensive*. He thinks, *This is how the story is supposed to happen*.

He also singled out *The Princess Bride* as a film that didn't compromise:

> That's a movie where they didn't make it good by the people's standards. They didn't try to incorporate a bunch of silly gimmicks to make people like it. It just was what it wanted to be.

. . . .

Can schools create a space big enough and free enough so that writers like Ernest can write the way they want to? Or do filters inevitably get in the way? Filters—grades, rubrics, requirements to use specific words or plot structures, limitations on the use of violence, comparisons to other students—that contaminate this space.

So we need to ask:

> Can we inhabit the dizzying worlds that Ernest and his friends create?

> Can we experience with them the dangers and narrow escapes?

> Can we even help them think through their plots, imagine their characters?

> Can we play their game?

It's a challenge worth taking up.

3

Fiction Versus Nonfiction

Or, Why I'd Rather Not Write
About Parking Meters

It's almost like an essay strips imagination from kids.

—Alyssa, eighth grader

My first interview with Ernest occurred early in his ninth-grade year, and I wanted to reconnect with him in tenth grade to see if his view of school writing had changed, and to catch up on whatever epic he was working on. So I caught him on a Saturday afternoon, just as he was getting home from a seven-hour shift at McDonald's.

His opinion hadn't changed: "They don't really emphasize creative writing. They tell you to do essays about *other people's* creative writing. Like, it's write an essay about a book rather than write a story." A recent assignment was to write about a dominant emotion in one of the characters in *The Crucible*—and he seemed to have a good bead on the topic, focusing on Reverend Parris and fear. But it was not particularly appealing: "I'd rather be writing the story that some kid does an essay on than being the kid that does an essay on someone else's story."

Ernest is rejecting what he sees as the subordinate role that writing assumes, particularly as students move through the grades. Writing is reduced to becoming a tool to explicate literature. Fiction, thus, holds a peculiar place in the curriculum—on the one hand it is central, the reading of it, that is. But the writing of it, for reasons we have already laid out, is rarely even a possibility. Writing is colonized, controlled, limited by its alpha twin, the reading curriculum.

This chapter explores student perceptions of the nonfiction writing they are required to do in school. Clearly, their attitudes toward nonfiction have been shaped by their school experience with it—although some have found a path to creative nonfiction, as we will see later. While many of them, by their own admission, were successful with this school-based writing, it was clear they didn't like it much. In some cases, they disliked the guidelines—what one student called *filters*—that undermine the pleasure they took in their self-sponsored writing. And in some cases, most in fact, they felt that nonfiction, by its very nature, imposed limits that they disliked. As one student said, the content of nonfiction is "set in concrete."

These students were also affected by forces like the Common Core State Standards that emphasized more objective, less personal forms of writing and reading. The pragmatic goal was to make students "college and career ready." This meant reading that stayed "within the four corners of the text," questions that were "text dependent," and writing that explicated texts and minimized emotion (Coleman and Pimentel 2011). A key creator of the CCSS, David Coleman was sharply critical of writing that stressed personal opinion and experience:

> The only problem, forgive me for saying this so bluntly, the only problem with those two forms of writing [reader responses or personal narratives] is as you grow up in this world you realize people really don't give a shit about what you feel or what you think. (2012)

Students wanted no part of this objectivity. They could play the game but were not invested in it.

A number of students identified this pragmatic focus—on "college and career readiness"—as a key factor in limiting writing options. Eve, an eleventh grader, cited the dominance of STEM in schools, which in her view turned even writing into a task where you were either right or wrong, similar to a math problem:

> When I write an essay they're either right or wrong. They're passing or they're failing, and the thing with creative writing is that there's no right or wrong, it's expression left to interpretation. I think that they not only don't know how to assess creative writing, but they want to have a more practical student, if that makes sense, because schools care so much about practicality and sending kids off to college and having good records. So everything is reduced.

Writing guides created by the U.S. Department of Education offer evidence for Eve's claim. Take, for example, this opening paragraph to a pamphlet published by the department's Institute of Education Sciences:

> Improving students' writing skills helps them succeed inside and outside the classroom. Effective writing is a vital component of students' literacy achievement, and writing is a critical communication tool for students to convey thoughts and opinions, describe ideas and events, and analyze information. Indeed, writing is a life-long skill that plays a key role in postsecondary success across academic and vocational disciplines. (2017, 1)

The key word is *success*—and who can argue with success? But what is missing from this claim? The entire realm of writing for self-expression and literary enrichment, or even a nod to the way that writing not only "communicates" thought but also creates it. Writing is a *tool* for success.

Eighth grader Doug adopted a more conspiratorial, quasi–Marxist point of view of the limitations of school writing:

> When you're a child, you're super-young and you, like, want to do all these different sorts of things. And school drills it out of you. Then they bring you to the guidance counselor and they're, like, "What do you want to do when you grow up" and you're, like, "Help me!"

I asked him how they drilled creativity out of students:

Like in math they teach you a strict way, how to solve a problem, and then they tell you to do it. In social studies you read out of the book, remember what you read, and put it down—it's really simple, straightforward sort of stuff. If they tried to do stuff that was more complex it would force kids to be more creative about what they do. But kids get used to doing the simple monotonous type of task.

In English classes, Doug believes they teach an inflexible type of academic writing "because they want to prepare you for college and into the workforce as soon as possible"—hardly an inviting place for his stories about Old Man Jenkins, a character he has been writing about for literally half of his life.

For Doug the very nature of nonfiction writing is limiting because it precludes invention or creation:

> In nonfiction everything has been done. Everything is known, right. You're just writing it down, what is fact, but with fiction you create fact.

Nonfiction, as he saw it, was simply an act of transposition, of taking from one source and putting it down, slightly modified.

Perhaps in my own day as a student, the finding of information was more of a challenge: all that work in card catalogues, the guides to periodical literature, note cards, time in library stacks, finding opposing views on a topic. But not today, as ninth grader Josie explains:

> Fiction writing can be whatever you want it to be. And that's something special that you don't get out of writing nonfiction or get out of writing a research paper. And as interesting as parking meters can be—which was not my favorite essay to write. I had to convince my teacher it was the most effective invention of the 1920s. It was not! That's fact, something that everyone knows or could know. You could look it up on Wikipedia and be, like, OK that's parking meters.

Josie did, however, do fairly extensive research on herbal medicine for her fan fiction dystopian novel.

The students I interviewed were regularly critical of what Janet Emig called the "Fifty Star Theme"—or the five-paragraph theme—that she saw as endemic in the late 1960s and early 1970s. It was, in her view, "so indigenously American" that one could imagine a backdrop with Kate Smith singing "God Bless America" or the piccolo obligato from "Stars and Stripes Forever" (1983, 93).

When students used the term *essay*, it was to this form they were referring. Here is how eleventh grader Natasha described it: "We're basically told the stuff to write in an essay and it's basically a formula." This kind of essay writing had become almost machine-like for her, which came in handy when she was running out of time on a midterm exam and down to twenty minutes to write:

> I ended up getting completely done because I know how it should be written and what you need. In the intro you need a hook, your thesis, and what the book is about. And the rest is just, "OK what's you point in the paragraph? Explain it. What's your point in the next paragraph? Explain it." So, in a way, the basic essay is just one formula that you need to get memorized and once you do it, it's kind of simple.
>
> We're basically told the stuff to write in essays and it's basically a formula. And if kids think that's the only way they can write, that might discourage them from wanting to write. If you give them a chance to write what they want and to show the creative side they might have a lot more fun because they can use their imagination and it's not just some formula that they're following to make some essay presentable. It's their own imagination coming to life in front of them.

This matches the description by Eve:

> An essay is black and white and you have your points and you just make it a success by stating "this is true and here's why." In a school setting it's hard to try creative nonfiction without thinking you're going in the wrong direction.

It also matches an observation by a Florida researcher who found beginning teachers were expected to take a "scientific" approach: writing was viewed as a product that could be objectively assessed according to explicit criteria—clearly with an eye on standardized tests (Kohnen 2019).

I encountered the five-paragraph theme in high school around 1965, and I later traced the source to Lucile Vaughan Payne's guide, *The Lively Art of Writing* (1965), though I expect it preexisted her book. Her version of the essay was highly structured. The opening paragraph was an inverted pyramid—with the writer moving from general to specific (often leading to vapid opening sentences), followed by three body paragraphs, and then a conclusion paragraph where the pyramid was upright, and the writer moved from specific to general. All this guidance often made the writing difficult, especially the pyramids—even as an eleventh grader I resented being jerked around this way. (The pyramids were actually featured on the cover of the first edition.) More recent diagrams of the essay have tended toward the hamburger.

In the half century since her book came out, this school essay model has been criticized extensively, and mocked by cartoonist Sandra Boynton, picturing it as a lumbering dinosaur with a head, three big humps, and a tail that went over ground that had already been covered. It has been challenged by advocates of the essay (not the school essay) like Katherine Bomer (2016) and by John Warner (2019), who rejects the compartmentalization of analytic and creative writing.

How to explain its indestructability? Well, it gets some things right, sort of. Essays, all writing really, *should* have a purpose or point, as should paragraphs (Don Murray would always challenge us with the question "What is this about?"). The opening sentence of paragraphs *should* guide the reader. Assertions *should* be followed by some kind of evidence. And for the inexperienced writer, or one for whom organization is a cognitive problem, the rigid structure can be a lifeline, what my colleague Christina Ortmeier-Hooper has called a "survival genre." Some of the students I interviewed also explained that paradoxically the rigidity of the school essay, often defined by strict rubrics, made it useful for "objective" grading, while fiction writing did not fit as well, or at all. It's very openness was an assessment problem.

What we can call the school essay is often justified by the claim that you need to learn the rules before you can break them. Presumably the "rules" are this five-paragraph structure—which makes me think of something we would say on the playground when someone would proclaim a "rule." We would say, "Says who?"

These so-called rules are not derived from any study of what essay writers actually do—essays have been an open, fluid form since Montaigne began writing them in his tower in the 1580s. And from the beginning they have been a personal form, open to humor, anecdote, voice, even digression. If we are to derive any "rule" from a study of essays it would be that essays are animated by the personality and thought process of the writer. Even when the *I* is not present, we as readers can sense the engagement, the cognitive energy, of the writer.

I would also be a bit more sympathetic to this argument—learn the rules before you break the rules—if instruction really got to the break-the-rules part. In fact, even if the goal is the pragmatic one of college preparation, writers will need a repertoire of moves to write the more extensive kinds of writing they are expected to do. It's really not about breaking the rules but using the tools. It's about finding a way to feel personally connected, even when the topic feels originally distant.

It is entirely possible to reinvent some of the traditional, and often tired, types of assignments, such as the informational report. Grayson described how in seventh grade they had to research and report on a famous person, but instead of just writing out researched facts, they became "wax figures" in a sort of museum, and would impersonate their character and give a pre-pared speech (he was Harry Houdini). Other classmates would spend their monopoly money to hear this speech. Grayson felt that modification of the "report" made it presentational and entertaining.

Some writers do this modifying themselves. Which brings me to a story Eve told me. In eighth grade her class was given one of the most un-promising of assignments, a manual-type description of a process, how to make or do something.

> I thought, this is going to be terrible. This is going to be "How to Make a Sandwich"—and that's what the other kids did. I cannot do that. I cannot spend hours of my life writing about how to make a sandwich. So what I did, as soon as we were assigned it, I remember getting out of my chair and going up to my English teacher—I loved my English teacher, by the way, and I asked her, "Could I do an informative paper on 'How to Be Eve'?" And she goes, "as long as you have what's required."
>
> So I wrote it, "How to Be Eve." How to dress like Eve, how to act like Eve, and I actually made the intro very funny, "If you're having a midlife crisis or need a Halloween costume, then becoming Eve is just for you." It was funny like that. When we did peer review, I showed it to about four people, and they were laughing and showing it to their friends.

Eve's experience with this how-to essay closely parallels the account Russell Baker gave in his memoir, *Growing Up* (1982). In an episode that I would regularly read aloud to my students, Baker describes his dread of having to write an essay for his eleventh-grade English teacher, the very prim and proper Mr. Fleagle. He delayed as long as he could and finally looked through the list of possible topics where he was struck by one, "The Art of Eating Spaghetti":

> This title produced an extraordinary sequence of mental images. Surging out of the depths of memory came a vivid recollection of a night at Belleville when all of us were seated around the supper table—Uncle Allen, my mother, Uncle Charlie, Doris, Uncle Hal—and Aunt Pat served spaghetti, and none of the adults had enough experience to be good at it. (187–88)

Suddenly Baker wanted to write about "the warmth and good feeling of it, but I wanted to put it down simply for my own joy, not for Mr. Fleagle." He realized that writing it as he wanted would violate all the rules of proper essay writing. So he decided to write about it for his own pleasure and then write a proper essay after that. But he never got to write that proper essay and had to hand in his account of eating spaghetti with his family.

Two days after he passed it in, Mr. Fleagle passed back the essays, all but Baker's, an ominous sign. Instead Fleagle chose to read his essay aloud to the class:

> And he started to read. My words! He was reading *my words* out loud to the entire class. What's more, the entire class was listening. Listening attentively. Then someone laughed, then the entire class was laughing, not in contempt and ridicule, but with openhearted enjoyment. Even Mr. Fleagle stopped two or three times to repress a small prim smile. (188)

Thus began Baker's illustrious career as an essayist.

We can draw the same teaching lesson from these two stories—the value of what one student called "wiggle room." Both teachers were open to something that they couldn't have expected when they gave the assignment; each allowed for what Anne Dyson (2016) has called permeability, a meeting of school requirements with the personal themes and interests of the student. Outside meets inside. Both Eve and Baker found a way to transform the assignment in a way that made it personal, creative, and interesting to readers (and themselves). The necessity of "owning" an assignment became a credo for Eve: "Anything I write I try to have a purpose, try to have it reflect me in some way. I try to make it interesting, meaningful to me."

Eve's experience was not, however, one where, as she moved on in school, she could "break the rules." She found they became more rigid. I spoke with her in a local library long into the evening, and our interview seemed to come to an end. I stopped the tape, but she and her mother indicated that she had more to say. I turned the tape back on and she described how profoundly alienated she was from the writing expected of her, to the point where she dropped out of AP and found her honors class no longer inviting—she was getting Cs. She felt "shut down."

> English is such a broad thing and they're finding ways to shrink it, to make it "right," like a math problem with one answer. It's being so censored and uniformal that it has to be one way. It's hard to be practical when it doesn't feel like there is a meaning because I always like to be doing things for myself and affecting others— and you're writing about all the foreshadowing in *Julius Caesar* and it doesn't feel like I get the chance to be creative myself.

When I asked her about this broader view of English, she saw storytelling as central, whether fiction or nonfiction:

> Creative writing is what holds humanity together. You can build a prosthetic with your STEM—that is amazing. But the core of humanity is through storytelling, and writing, and just being around people, embracing our differences, sharing our views and our feelings. Creativity is what brings us together and creative writing is a form of that.

Storytelling to the Rescue

In the first chapter of *The Adventures of Huckleberry Finn*, Huck describes what it is like to eat at the Widow Douglas' home:

> When you got to the table you couldn't go right to eating, but you had to wait for the widow to tuck down her head and grumble a little over the victuals, though there warn't really anything the matter with them—that is, nothing only everything was cooked by itself. In a barrel of odds and ends

it is different; things get mixed up, and the juice kind of swaps
around, and the things go better. (Twain 1885, 2)

The same holds true for genres of writing—things go better when the juices
are swapped, when story and information and argument are not seen as distinct types of writing, as "boxes."

I have previously argued (Newkirk 2014) that narrative is the *primary*
way in which we understand ourselves and the world, it is the genre of genres.
Even the communication of scientific information works better with narrative. In fact, according to a recent article in the *Proceedings of the National
Academy of Sciences*, "narrative cognition is thought to represent the default
mode of human thought, providing structure to reality and serving as the
underlying foundation for memory":

> This reliance on narratives is suggested to be the result of an
> evolutionary benefit because narratives provide their users with
> a format of comprehension to simulate possible realities, which
> would serve to better predict cause-and-effect relationships
> and model the thoughts of other humans in the complex social
> interactions that define our species. (Dahlstrom 2014)

This is a powerful claim, that narrative understanding is a basic evolutionary adaptation. And it is a welcome one, because it seems to bridge
the practical and the creative—a false dichotomy, as a number of students
pointed out.

According to senior Keelyn, schools miss out on bringing storytelling into subject areas; she advocated a narrative-across-the-curriculum approach. I asked her how this would work in social studies and she described
how she wrote a historical fiction piece on the Vietnam War:

> I wrote from the point of view of a soldier who had been
> drafted unwillingly, and he was there, and he was sensitive, and
> he just wants to go home and write. I did a little background
> research and it helped me understand and learn about that time
> period. I learned how terrible it was, what a struggle it was. Just
> kind of exploring the emotions, some pretty crazy things. I could
> see, "Oh that's why they came back with PTSD. This is why the
> Vietnam War is looked down upon. Or this is why the soldiers
> weren't celebrated when they came back, weren't honored." They
> were drafted against their will and it was definitely protested.

> You learn historical content but a more personal connection. Even though it's not real you're exploring their emotions and what they are going through. It gives you a deeper understanding of the human experience.

Using research in this way also solves the problem of mere transposition, of merely repackaging information from some source into "reports."

Caroline, an eighth-grade novel writer, admitted that doing research and then putting it all "in your own words" can be tedious, but she had the "wiggle room" to include fictional elements in her report on puffins. She conveyed the information by following an imaginary fifteen-year-old puffin that she called Siefur, who is searching for food off the coast of Iceland:

> A black shape propels itself through the water, flapping its wings every now and then for a boost, and rotating its little orange webbed feet to steer. Followed by six of his friends, Seifur ventures deeper into the shallow waters near the huge breeding colony on Vestmannaeyjar. Although Atlantic Puffins are able to dive up to 200 feet, they would rather search for their tasty morsels in shallow water, and less than 10 miles from their colony. Moments ago, before he had dived, Seifur had pressed his feathers tight to his body, releasing the air kept underneath. Whenever puffins dive, they cannot have any air trapped beneath their feathers, otherwise they would float.

Even the opening sentence of her report vividly places the reader on this island in the North Sea: "To the southwest of mainland Iceland sits a group of islands, where the sea tosses and turns restlessly, and the wind whips one's face till it turns bright red."

These narrative skills are profoundly functional; they help the reader retain the information by making it visible. In his book *The Sense of Style* (2014), Steven Pinker reminds us how central sight is for humans; a huge proportion of our brains is devoted to it. A nonvisual writing style, as you sometimes get in academic writing, is hard to stay with. We comprehend much better when the writer "shows the events making up the subject matter transparently, by narrating an unfolding plot with real characters doing things" (48–49). Which is what Caroline did.

And not surprisingly, David Coleman was wrong about giving a shit about feelings. We are primed to remember information, events, and experiences that in some way arouse us, particularly if that emotion is related to fear or threat (Schacter 2001, 181). In the case of trauma, victims can be haunted by the persistence of a memory. Here again there are obvious evolutionary roots—recalling threatening situations has clear survival value (which is why we often seem to recall bad experiences more vividly than good ones).

Readers are more likely to remember information if it has some emotional weight; for example, if it explores social issues by showing how they affect real people with whom we can identify. Since all narrative plots involve some form of trouble, they have the potential to hold our attention and find a place in our long-term memory. As one student put it, "In nonfiction you need action to make it nonbland." Put another way, the tools of creative nonfiction are *profoundly functional* in helping readers hold on to information. Feelings matter.

One question I asked students in all interviews was whether they thought fiction writing helped them with the other kinds of writing they were expected to do. Students often mentioned the way it could foster a love of writing, voice, skills in word choice, and the mechanics of writing. But eighth grader Adarsh felt it had a close parallel to argumentative writing:

> You have to think about how other people react to situations. In my story I thought of how the dad would react to his daughter being beaten up, and that puts you in the mind of other people. You have to decide how they would react and if it would be reasonable or not. . . . You have to think from the minds of other people and their personalities.
>
> So it helps you look at something from different standpoints as well. Because you're writing from a character that you may not like—like in a persuasive essay you may be writing from a point of view that you don't agree with. So there's a kind of mini-correlation there.

Adarsh seems to be edging toward a position that Robert Frost once articulated: "Everything written is as good as it is dramatic. It need not declare itself in form, but it is drama or it is nothing" (quoted in Poirier 1997, 452). This clash of points of view occurs in fiction and argument, and even in informational writing we need some form of plotting to maintain our attention.

. . . .

In the early sixteenth century, the Dutch scholar Erasmus published a writing guide entitled *On Copia of Words and Ideas*. It became a huge best seller, a mega Strunk and White, going through eighty-five editions in his lifetime. *Copia* translates as "abundance." His book encourages constant practice and attempts to develop writers with a ready supply of language and material—something appropriate to say or write whenever the occasion arises. Erasmus draws on the work of the Roman rhetorician Quintilian (whose own writing text was a best seller) and a tradition of rhetoric "infused with the notions of expansiveness, amplification, abundance" (Crowley and Hawhee 2004).

One way to imagine *copia* is to witness its absence. In my early years of teaching, I assigned a response paper and set what I thought would be an easily attainable 500-word goal. It was in the prehistoric era of typewriting, and one student kept a word-count tally at intervals in the margin of his paper. The first was, as I recall, at about the 180-word mark, then the notations came closer together, 240, 310—then began to count after each sentence until he hit 439, which he decided was close enough. He was grinding it out, sentence by sentence. The problem may have been my assignment, which I have forgotten. But I also wondered if he had ever been in that psychological zone where writing seemed effortless, almost received and not composed, where sentence led to sentence, rather than straining for something to write.

Studies of the writing that goes on in U.S. schools confirm the picture that students describe in this chapter. Arthur Applebee and Judith Langer led a study of writing instruction in middle and high schools across the country that had strong reputations for teaching writing. They found examples of excellent, carefully planned instruction, which set demanding tasks for students. But on the whole, they found students rarely wrote more than a couple paragraphs for any assignment.

> The actual writing that goes on in typical classrooms across the country remains dominated by tasks in which the teacher does all the composing, and students are left only to fill in the blanks, whether copying directly from a teacher's presentation, completing worksheets and chapter summaries, replicating highly formulaic essay structures keyed to high stakes tests, or writing the information the teacher is seeking. (2011, 26)

Given these restrictions, it is hard to imagine how a student could ever experience that feeling of "abundance," of excess, of open space. And I would argue that until young writers have that feeling, they have no way of knowing the pleasures of composing.

My favorite question in my interviews went like this: "If I could be inside your head while you were writing, what would I see?" Students would often blink, then smile because I don't think they had ever been asked this question. ("It's total confusion!!!") Then they would go on to describe a deeply pleasurable process in the free space, overflowing with possibilities, *copia*, that they rarely experienced in school, and almost never with traditional nonfiction assignments.

In the next chapter we go inside with them.

4

The Writing Zone

If you were inside my head while I was walking and thinking about writing, you'd be crushed by the flow of ideas.

—Eighth grader Caroline

The first major "modern" novel was built, ironically, on the premise that reading was dangerous. The book concerns Alonso Quixano, a fifty-year-old Spanish nobleman who holes up in his library reading chivalric romances to the point of madness. He is unable to distinguish his fantasies from reality—he renames himself Don Quixote, his tired horse Rocinante (literally "no longer a working horse"), and the neighboring farm girl Dulcinea del Toboso. The books have such a powerful and disturbing effect on him that his housekeeper and the local priest go through his library, burning the most immoral ones—raising the interesting question of how the priest knew which ones they were. *Don Quixote* is fiction about the seduction of fiction.

But this danger, this capacity to enter the book—in the words of one student, to "be the book"—is the great attraction of fiction. In his classic study of reading, Jeffrey Wilhelm quotes a student describing this entry process:

It's like you're standing in line for the diving board on a windy day and you're freezing your nuts off. If you'll excuse the expression. [*Laughs*] Where was I? Oh yeah. It's like you're in pain and have your arms wrapped around you and the concrete is scratching your feet. The first part of the story is the line, and the ladder and the board. When everything comes together and you jump in it's like you're in this underwater world like INSTANTLY and then you stay down there and never come up until someone makes you. (1997, 55)

And what is it like to be submerged or, as Nancie Atwell's students term it, in "the reading zone"? Here is one student's description:

First of all you see what's happening in your head, like a movie screen. You care about the characters and think about what you would do at every point where they make a decision. You block out the sounds of the outside world. Eventually it doesn't even feel like you are reading. You don't seem to be actually reading the words as much as it is happening. (Atwell and Merkel 2016, 24)

One of the students I interviewed described her reading of the Divergent series in exactly the same way:

The way she [Veronica Roth] wrote I felt like I was there. I felt like I was either watching a movie while I was reading the book or I was in the story myself. It wasn't like I was just reading the words off the page. I was imagining it in my head. (Josie)

Psychologists would call this a description of *optimal experience*, of being in a state of flow, when we are being truly fluent, so fully engaged that we lose a sense of clock time and of our surroundings—so that we often feel disorientation when we have to shift back to the real world. It is a deeply pleasurable state that is its own reward—it may make us "college and career ready" but that is not why we are doing it. In the jargon of philosophy, it is autotelic, "having within itself the purpose of its existence or happening."

According to Atwell, a central characteristic of avid, passionate readers is the capacity to enter this zone, to find the conditions and authors that reliably invite them in. Reluctant readers, resistant readers, reader who can but don't, have never been there—and are often mystified by the devotion of other classmates to reading.

For me a turning point was reading one of the Chip Hilton series, a book called *Ten Seconds to Play* by Clair Bee. It was one of those series books like The Hardy Boys—predictable cliff-hangers at the end of each chapter. But I was lost in it—as I recall I finished it sitting at a picnic table in Mohican State Park while everyone else had started in on the hot dogs, chips, and inevitable fruit-cocktail Jell-O. I knew at the time I wanted to reenter that space. Years later, recalling how important it was for me, I found a copy—and found it unreadable.

Flow is not simply an effortless activity, though. The skilled skier does not experience it going down the bunny slope. But it is where we feel appropriately challenged—our capacities are activated, but we are not constantly aware of exerting ourselves. I believe skilled activity is misrepresented by much of the current talk about rigor and persistence. This is not to say hard work is not important, or that in performing any task there aren't moments when learners must consciously push themselves through difficulties. But the consciousness of exertion cannot be the predominant experience; rigor cannot be the primary bodily sensation.

William James makes an important distinction between voluntary and involuntary attention. In voluntary attention we are aware of willing ourselves to be more alert or productive. We tell ourselves to cease to daydream, to concentrate. We give ourselves pep talks. But voluntary attention can only occur in spurts. We are far more efficient (and happy) when we can sustain a state of involuntary attention, when we don't drift in and out, when we are not consciously exerting ourselves (James 1958, 78–79). That is when we can be in the reading zone, when we can "be the book."

This is the same distinction eighth grader Alyssa made when I asked her what advice she would give to other writers:

> I would definitely say work hard—but don't push yourself too hard. You have to be in the zone to do it. You don't want to work yourself too hard so that all your imagination is gone and you're writing strictly because there is a due date. You want to write because you enjoy it and because you are putting your heart and soul into this and you're writing something you want to write about. And if you're working yourself so hard that's not going to happen, and you're going to run out of ideas and your story is

going to end up bland. You need to give yourself breaks so that you can really think of something new and then you can write it down when you're doing this.

These intervals allow her unconscious to aid her composing. Psychologist Graham Wallas argues that in creative thinking there should be "an interval free from conscious thought on the particular problem concerned. . . ." and that these intervals are times of "mental relaxation" (quoted in Britton et al. 1977, 29). Alyssa put it this way:

> You can just be spacing out in class and you can get a great idea. Or in the middle of the night I would wake up at 3 in the morning—and it's like I have a great idea. But sometimes you don't get a great idea for hours on end until random parts of the day or night.

In this chapter we explore this writing zone.

Pleasure and Work

It may be harder to enter a writing zone, a deeply pleasurable state of engagement, comparable to the reading zone. Writing is slower, both in the mechanics of composing, and the need for intervals of invention (and rest). Compared to the fluidity of reading or speaking, writing "is but a line that moves haltingly across the page, exposing as it goes, all that the writer doesn't know, then passing into the hands of a stranger . . ." (Shaughnessy 1977, 7). Readers, by contrast, can stay in their zone, attending and reacting as they choose, hidden and safe.

Yet the writers I interviewed found that zone, often on their own, often away from school, often inverting the rules of school. As one student put it, "School is your job as a kid." It was work, and writing was presented as work. But the fictional space they described was open and playful. Natasha, an eleventh grader, identifies a fifth-grade ghost story as her turning point. The story, she acknowledges, was not unusual—friends talking about a ghost that turns out to be real and friendly:

> I was really happy when I was writing it but I didn't realize how happy I was until I finished it. What made me happy was that

it was an idea from my mind, my own creation come to life. My imagination was right here in front of me. That was such a cool feeling, such a neat thing to see. Just this random idea that popped into my head come to fruition.

Other writers would also regularly use the words *imagination* and *creativity* and almost always *freedom* to describe the sensation of working in this zone. In the interviews we began to unpack those terms.

Open Space

Heck, I want to write a book.

Caroline, on writing her first picture book

A central theme in almost all the interviews was a craving for open space—unrestricted by formula, rubric, grading, comparison to other students, or the limitation of stubborn factuality. A surprising number of writers didn't even share their writing widely, as even accommodating an audience could be an interfering "filter." As Eva put it:

It's like seeing something that you think is beautiful and everyone thinks is ugly—and not caring that other people think it's ugly, only that you think it's beautiful.

Many describe the exhilarating opportunity to create worlds, invent characters, make choices:

It's fun to create your own thing and see what other people created. Like you're free to do whatever you want, if you know what I mean. You don't have friends—make your own. You want to live in a world different from your own—make your own. It feels like being a god or something—you're free to create. (Caroline)

I've always been curious about things I can't know. Creating a world I can be part of is cool because I created it. You can do whatever you want. It doesn't just follow the rules of the earth. I know that sounds weird. But you can have someone getting lost

on the moon. It can be some magical world—like Narnia when the
kids go through the closet door and end up in another dimension.
You can create anything. (Caitlyn)

Ninth grader Josie framed this desire for freedom in advice she had for
teachers:

> I would say don't let kids think they have to censor what
> they write. I mean, it's fiction, it can be whatever you want.
> Sometimes when you say, "It can't be this or it can't be like that."
> Like "Go write a piece of fiction but I'm going to judge you on
> how creative it is and how realistic the setting is."
>
> I've read some of my friend's writing and "This could be so
> good but I know what the teacher is looking for and you're trying
> to put that in the story." Don't give anybody a rubric in fiction
> writing—"setting," "character," "plot." Let them have at it—and see
> what comes of it.

Josie was clear that this didn't mean that anything goes in a story—
each sets its own requirements. And in one of hers she researched medicinal
herbs, and where they grew, to use them properly in the story.

The position I kept hearing students articulate seemed consistent with
what Katie Wood Ray called "the immediate release of responsibility model"
(2015, 112). Her term subverts a very popular model of instruction first defined by David Pearson and Margaret Gallagher, "the gradual release of responsibility model [GRR]" (1983). In this GRR approach there is a great deal
of preteaching, modeling, scaffolding—before the student is "released" to
more independent work. And as Ray admits, this makes sense when asking
young children to do something as complicated as making books:

> Surely something as complicated as bookmaking should require
> some awesome feat of teaching to get it started. And surely—
> as complicated as writing and illustrating are—this teaching
> feat should start with one small step accompanied by lots of
> teacher guidance at first, and not by an immediate release of
> responsibility. Surely. (Ray 2015, 112)

Well, not so surely. Ray shows that "giving children complete control of
their own decision-making positions them as bookmakers on this first day
and across the year" (112). Children dove in, rarely doubting that they had

the capacity to make books, aided along the way by their teacher, but not controlled (or "released") by her.

The students I interviewed wanted free space, and they often found guidelines, established plot structure, and rubrics to be interference, what one writer called "filters." All of them had been swimming in fiction—songs, movies, video games, cartoons, TV shows, and, yes, books—for their entire conscious lives. It was not a foreign territory that needed to be modeled. I asked Caroline about advice for writers new to fiction:

> Do it. Don't wait until someone makes you do it. Just do it. A lot of people are stopped because they think they're not good enough to write. Well, you're not going to get better unless you start writing.

Caitlyn had similar advice for teachers, supporting the "immediate release of responsibility" model:

> Don't tell kids what to write—let them figure it out for themselves. You can give them maybe a sentence or two to start them off—maybe a word to start off. But don't make them base it on one thing. Let them expand and go where they want to be. Don't keep them on the railroad track—go off the tracks. Don't be scared. You can't write something too dark. You can't write something too happy. If you have a dark sense of writing just go for it, just embrace it. Don't be scared about it. If you want to write happy stories embrace that too.

I asked her what kind of "railroad tracks" limited students. She mentioned being required to use certain words or strict rules about staying on a topic:

> If you are writing about an apple, you could not write about a pear or a banana—it has to be about the apple.

These writers could often point to useful advice, prompts, planning tips, and motivating forms of encouragement—one, a lover of horror stories (who is actually named after a character in a horror movie), appreciated her teacher saying, "Write me a story that will keep me up at night." So the role of the teacher is not passive, but it is responsive to the intentions of the writer—and doesn't predetermine them. It's like the teacher could get on a moving train. Later, we will look more directly at how teachers can help.

The Pleasure of Chaos

No student I interviewed was as deliberate or excessive as Ernest, with his 100 generated names for his great epic, but many described the pleasure of so many possibilities, and the chaos in their minds. According to Caroline, if I could be inside her head when she was walking, and thinking of her story, I would be "crushed by the flow of ideas." Samara, another eighth grader, said we would see a "mess" in her brain.

NaNoWriMo writer Grayson described his own frustration in what he saw as a district model of three to four nonfiction assignments a year. The chance to write fiction was a huge relief:

> I'd go ballistic because I'd be so happy to finally get something I wanted to write about. I'd get my topic and by the time I started writing there would be something completely different because my brain would just run wild and I would just get to explore the different possibilities of what I could write about instead of being confined to one topic.
>
> It's chaos, honestly, because I'd be writing one thing, thinking another thing, and planning for a different thing.
>
> A lot of my teachers would give me a chart plan to my stories. If I had a paper shredder, I'd shred them. I never went with the plan.

Students described a rich swirl of possibilities, "chaos," "a jumble of thoughts":

> Usually my mind is going a mile a minute. I've developed the middle of the story and my hand is trying to keep up and get there. (Keelyn)

When I asked eighth grader Ben for a tour of his brain, he responded:

> You would probably see a lot of confusion, a lot of not quite knowing what to do, but still going for it. I keep thinking of all

these possibilities and I'm confused about how to pick one to focus on.

I mentioned that *confusion* is usually perceived negatively, but Ben didn't seem to see it that way. He added, "I don't because it allows me to power through."

Kayla describes herself as someone with a "track record of having trouble in school," in no small part due to her ADHD, which causes her to "space out," particularly in math classes. I asked her if, like Ernest, she found her "disability" to be an advantage in writing fiction:

> That's how I feel. My mind will go a million miles an hour. I'm always jumping around to different ideas but because of that I'll be able to come up with so many different ideas rather than being stuck in a single track way of thinking.
>
> It makes it so that I can say "this is how it is" and "this is how it is" and "this is how it is" and there are so many things I can draw from. I'm thinking about so many things and observing so many things. I observe more things than the average person does at one time—and that's just because I'm everywhere. That helps me.

These writers differed in their views on the usefulness of advanced planning, but what they all seemed to have in common was their planning "in the moment." I would ask them about an original plot twist, or a particularly effective ending, and it was rarely planned well ahead. This sense of improvisation was one of the pleasures of fiction writing: possibilities became apparent in the writing. They may not have all wanted to shred planning charts, but they weren't tied to them.

My colleague and friend Don Murray spent his life collecting quotes from writers, and so many of them stressed the importance of surprise and decision-making within the process of writing. Here, for example, is playwright Neil Simon:

> You have to have an idea but you don't really know where it's going. You may sorta have a vision of what the play's to be like, but you don't really know what the second act is going to be about. In *Brighton Beach* I didn't know the second act was going to open with the father's heart attack, but when I got there that's what presented itself to me. I have to surprise

myself when I'm writing because I think if you know everything
that's coming and then write it out, the audience will see what's
coming too. (in Murray 1990, 112)

As the bumper sticker (quoting Tolkien) reminds us, "Not all who wander
are lost."

When I asked Josie to describe her process, it closely paralleled Simon's.
She was working on a twenty-four-chapter extension of the postapocalyptic
TV series *The Hundred*. She felt the director "majorly screwed up the plot and
characters" at the end of season 5. "It didn't feel true to who they were so I
was, like, 'I'll finish the season for you.'" I asked her what pleasure she took
from such a big project:

> I think it's most because I don't even know how I'm supposed to
> end a chapter. I try to end with a cliff-hanger, not "They lived
> happily ever after. The End." So I'll end one chapter and it's like
> "I don't even know what I'm supposed to do." It's usually I'll sit
> down and I'm going to write something and I have a general
> foggy idea of the first scene and then something in the scene
> clicks and I know what's going to happen.

She described how this process works in a chapter she shared with me:

> Like I'll be writing the beginning of this chapter and she [the
> main character] is shot in the side and I don't know what's going
> to happen. She can't die because she is the main character, and
> she can't exactly just recover, like, "I'm OK."

This situation pushed Josie to invent scenes where there is a search for
herbal cures, involving for her research to determine if the herbs could be
found in the place where her main character is injured.

The Cinematic I/Eye

Almost all the students I interviewed were avid readers, but when I asked
them about influences and models for their writing, they were just as likely
to be songs, video games, movies, and, as with the case of Josie, TV series.
If they mentioned books, they were rarely the ones assigned in school, many
of which they found slow-moving (*My Antonia* was singled out by some of

them). Often they likened the act of composing to transcribing a movie that they were simultaneously watching and directing—even acting in, as a character. One of the deep pleasures, then, is the sensation of receiving or viewing the unfolding story, rather than strenuously composing it.

As I expected, Ernest had a lot to say about this: "100 percent, 100 percent. All my ideas for books I see as movies."

> I'm typically watching the story and, like, also jotting down notes of what I predict will happen. It's kind of like I'm watching a movie and then you see something and you're like "I saw that and I think that's foreshadowing that this is going to happen." But the thing is, I'm also the director of the movie so I can actually make what I thought was foreshadowed happen. So most of the foreshadowing happens because I wrote the part and later in the story something big happens but that big thing happens because I got the idea from a small thing happening before.
>
> Whenever I write I always imagine it happens before me. Like I can see the characters, what they're going through—happiness, sadness. I can see all the fight scenes. They're all perfectly choreographed when I watch them.

Eighth grader Owen describes a slightly different visual process. I asked my typical question of what I would see if I was in his brain while he was writing:

> Well, you'd see lots of ideas flying by and then there's this big video screen, I guess, and some guy's sitting in front of it—and he's deciding whether that's a good idea or not and then the appropriate section of the brain to put it.

It is as if the movie screen becomes an internalized cognitive tool. The great Russian psychologist Lev Vygotsky, drawing on the work of Friedrich Engels, saw cultural tools as more than a means for controlling one's environment; they also alter the mental landscape of the user, creating "new natural conditions of existence" (Engels, quoted in Vygotsky 1978, 132). Take the clock. It helps us regulate and coordinate our activity, but it also becomes internalized, and we experience time in terms of hours and minutes (and not the position of the sun). It's actually hard for us to imagine time in any other way. In the same way, the movie, for many of these writers, is both a model of what they might create and also an internalized tool that helps them create it.

Visualization often helps Kayla launch a scene. As an example, she describes how she began one of her cowritten novels:

> It opens with a scene of they're in a conference room and they're talking about business economics and how it's going. And while writing it I saw the conference room and this white table and these folding chairs, and these people sitting on these folding chairs, slumped over because it's five in the morning and light is streaming from slats, from the sun. These visuals will come and a scene will be built in my head and from there I'll write the action of the characters, where this goes.

This account seems to parallel William Faulkner's famous description of how *The Sound and the Fury* was triggered by the image of a girl in a pear tree, with a muddy seat (in Murray 1990, 84).

Caitlyn described her own highly visual process of writing "Hunter," an account of a girl dealing with the grief of losing her father to cancer and, in an attempt to heal, revisiting a part of the woods near her house where she would go with him:

> I like how I describe everything so deeply. When I was imagining it I had a certain image in my head and, like, scenes in my head and I wrote it the way it sounds, exactly like I can see it in my head—like when she was first walking into the woods and she was surrounded by trees. I can picture that in my head.

I asked her to read that paragraph to me:

> I look around, and take in the sunrise filled woods I had been too anxious to even look at for four years. I took a deep breath, and slowly place my right foot, and then my left, on the fallen orange leaves. I hear a crunch, and embrace the fresh earthy smell that comes from beneath me. I had been afraid for too long to be reminded of my father, and now, in the midst of these trees I feel as if he is standing right next to me. The trees surround me, and as I exhale I feel overwhelmed.

In her dreamy state, she loses track of her dog.

It is difficult to overstate the importance of action in so many of the stories I read. They often seemed more movie-like than literary, and like Ernest, some of the writers aspired to be screenwriters. As I noted earlier they not once cited required school novels as models for their work—because they moved too slowly, bogged down in detail, slow off the mark. This criticism recalled for me a conversation I had with the young adult writer Carolyn Coman soon after her powerful novel *What Jaime Saw*, a Newbury Honor Book, was published. We were at a local park, and she mentioned that for her next book, she thought she would write a book that her own middle school son might actually read.

He was sitting right next to us and he sighed, "Great, but not fifty pages about the next five minutes of your life."

Eighth grader Adarsh begins his story "The Chase" with a vivid description of two older boys terrifying a young girl:

> Adam and I chase my sister through the lime-green grass, brandishing fake knives. The grass blades smash under our feet in a clump as I pursue her. She looks back, almost trips, and she screams even louder, probably at our GhostFace masks. I grip the fake knife in my hand and thrust it forward suggestively. I'm honestly enjoying this.

He described for me his strategy with this opening:

> I like to jump in with action, as you can see with "The Chase." I feel like action is a bit more involving to the reader. The reader in my opinion likes action books and I'm influenced by my own tastes—I like action too. Just the constant threat of something being there that you have to get rid of or you have to resolve. It provokes you to do stuff that the reader won't expect—unpredictability.

His opening does provoke us to wonder what kind of brother would go so far over the line to scare his sister. We're in.

Zach, a novel writer, is also a cinematic composer. When I asked him about what was going on his head when he wrote, he responded:

> You would see a whole lot of thoughts about how I could make this more exciting—or make this more interesting for the reader,

more enjoyable—more adventure, more excitement, that's what was going on in my head.

In his novel *3515 Mali Street*, there is an extended scene where the main character, Kyle, is tied up and imprisoned in a room. A central action of the story revolves around the hours that Kyle painfully tries to untie the ropes around his wrists. Eventually, he finds a nail and loosens them:

> Kyle was drained of energy. He had been trying to untie the knots on his wrists for hours now, and was just a few loops from finishing the last one. The rope was now loose enough for Kyle to just untie it with his hands. He had grown muscle memory on untying the rope and knew the exact pattern. He slowly grabbed the rope with his right hand and tugged on it, using the pattern, "Pull up, to the side, grab under, pull down. Pull up, to the side, grab under, pull down." It was a good minute before the rope became completely loose, releasing his wrists. The air hit his warm wrist and the cuts on it. It felt good, relieving. Kyle could finally reach the ground with his left hand and turn that side of his body.

I asked Zach about the process of writing this key scene:

> I would paint a picture in my head and I actually drew a picture of the room—and just kept thinking of different props in the room that could help him get untied, like the nail. And I really wanted that to be the main focus, that after all the struggles, he still made it through and survived. So I spent a lot of time on that part.

Although the term *imagination* has taken on the broader connotation of any kind of inventiveness or creativity, its root meaning is to form an image or a picture in the mind. Which is the deeply pleasurable process so many of these writers described.

The Zone

The writers I interviewed differed in how they felt about their final products, and who might read them. Some posted them on Wattpad and Archives of

Our Own, some shared with parents, some with a few friends, surprisingly few shared in school with classmates, even when the writing was supported by the school. What they all had in common, I feel, was the enjoyment of being in "the writing zone," of entering the movie theatre of their own minds, and accounting for what they see. I asked Kayla about why she wrote fiction, and it had little to do with audience, even finishing:

> I think it's the fact that I can go into this and write it and this is a really cool piece—and I think it is less about enjoying it after and more about enjoying the process and me being able to say, "This is a cool idea. I just want to get it out of my head and turn it into something."

I would argue that finding this zone is the central condition of engagement in writing—experiencing the sensation of open space and that flood of ideas in the brain, of launching out on a story without a clear itinerary. Or as Doc says at the end of *Back to the Future*, "Roads?! Where we're going, we don't need roads!!!"

Fiction writers describe this zone as a space where the story takes on a life of its own—similar to my interviewees watching a movie in their minds. Characters seem to have a will of their own, as Joyce Carol Oates describes:

> My characters really dictate themselves to me. I am not free of them, really, and I can't force them into situations they haven't themselves willed. They have the autonomy of characters in a dream. (in Murray 1990, 110)

And this experience is not limited to novel writing—I would argue that for all longer projects, fiction or nonfiction, there comes a point when you have to cease planning and researching. You have to stop reading and start writing, trusting that the project will teach you how to do the project. The pleasure of writing comes from the discovery and surprise that happen.

That has been my own experience. Years ago I spent several months writing a book on boys literacy. It mixed my own story as a boy, interviews with writers, research on gender, the experience of being a father. The more I worked on it the more things connected to the project—I would open the newspaper and find material. Everything stuck.

I distinctly remember the day I finished it. I remember where I was sitting, the final quote from a young writer, like those in this book, who was planning a twelve-chapter epic. I knew I was near the end and was expecting to feel some relief. There would still be the usual revision, the tedious copyediting—and search for dozens of references I was too busy or lazy to include. But the big work was done.

But what I felt was loss. I would never again have the same relationship I had with the book, getting up in the morning with a general idea of the next step, but so often surprised by an unexpected connection, or anecdote. A word would trigger a memory and I would run with it.

I understood that I would no longer have that feeling with the book. There might be book talks, and the pleasure of holding it in my hands, finally. But the partnership was over. I felt like a good friend was leaving town.

That is the zone that keeps us all wanting to write.

5

Going Deep
Fiction and Psychological Insight

I love flaws.

—Adarsh

Every family has legends, stories told and retold, embellished along the way. In our family these stories often focus on something foolish I have done. One in particular is about watermelons.

I am a great watermelon fan, and believe the agronomist who invented seedless watermelons, Hitoshi Kihara, should have statues and parades in his honor. So . . . each summer at our teachers institute we had picnics, often with watermelon as dessert. For one picnic I was in charge of ordering the watermelons from Sam's Club. I calculated how much I would eat and multiplied it by the number of teachers attending. It came out to twenty, or five of the hefty four packs you could get at Sam's.

I suspect you can guess the rest of the story. The teachers ate a total of four melons. I tried to see if any would take a four-pack home, but no one did. So I loaded the remaining sixteen watermelons into my car, took them home, and informed my family that we were on a mission to finish them before they went bad. Watermelon, I insisted, could go with *any* meal, not to mention it was a good snack.

We didn't quite make it. We had two rotting carcasses in the basement that I had to dispose of, but that was surely the summer of watermelon.

One reason this story persists in our family, I think, is that it is a kind of fable, with a lesson. Namely, how easy it is to be locked into our own mindset and to assume others share it. How hard to imagine that there are people who, at a summer picnic, will pass up on watermelon. Of course, Piaget noted that egocentrism is a basic trait of children, but we never outgrow it—and to imagine the consciousness of someone else is always difficult. But also critical for moral behavior—and for fiction writing.

Fiction writing provides a testing ground for practical psychological explorations in identity, in human flaws and pathologies, in the extremes of emotions—and darkness. One of the students I interviewed, eighth grader Samara was actually named after a character in the horror series *The Ring* who could burn images onto the minds of others. Samara is fascinated by the psychology of serial killers, and in her stories she explores how people experience fear in different ways. Adrash described for me how he created a main character who was an "egotist," looking down on other people and blaming any problem on what others have done. High school senior Keelyn selectively uses her own "better" traits to create her characters. A colleague of mine who teaches at UNH's summer Writers Academy, has an "alter ego day" where her students come in as an alternative self, maybe an opposite of the self they present normally.

The novelist Gayle Brandeis recommends that writers should give themselves a sort of psychological scratch test as if they were checking for an allergy, but in this case the writer is checking for things they have a strong reaction to. For example:

- my deepest fears
- social and political issues that break my heart
- places that repel me
- the qualities that annoy me most in people
- smells and tastes that make me sick
- objects that creep me out

She advises: "When you inject your own fears into the world of your story, when you allow yourself to enter your own shadow, your own darkness on the page, your story will take on a more mythic journey than you ever could imagine. . . ." (in Baty 2004, 117).

It might be argued that nonfiction, and the personal essay in particular, can also be a space for psychological exploration—which is of course true. The personal essay is sometimes seen as more "authentic" than student fiction, which can be so tied to popular media. But authenticity is a tricky claim. Even in the personal essay the writer is performing a role that involves revelation and withholding. In the college admission essay, writers often feel—justifiably—that they must tell a story of development in which they have grown by overcoming obstacles (see Vidali 2007; Wight 2017). Not a bad thing to write about but hardly free space.

The writers I interviewed turned this "authenticity" argument on its head and claimed fiction gives a wider space for psychological exploration. It is, for example, difficult to see how writers can explore real deviance—real evil—without the option of fiction. In many cases students' own sense of self, their own emotional makeup, becomes a tool, a baseline, for extrapolation or inversion.

Ethan, another Stephen King acolyte, offered me a fully developed explanation of how the horror works—distinguishing it from the violence that can become routine in some stories. Horror is more about mental states:

> The ways you can use violence where it really won't work is if the story is hollow. That's all there is. There is no other conflict. The whole thing is one big conflict that never gets resolved—or it's one big conflict that gets resolved at the end but the resolution isn't good. Say the entire thing's a war—and the war ends with a peace treaty. Like everybody says, "Yeah, what about a peace treaty?" And everything's good now. There would have to be other suspense, that can't be the only conflict. Like with Ky [the main character in a story], there is mental conflict—he's asking, "What is happening to me?" He goes and eats his aunt and uncle because something is telling him to. He doesn't want to. The mental pressure is so intense that that's when he breaks down and that's when the violence comes in. But before that it is mostly mental.

But in order to do this, the writer has to accept—and use—thought patterns they would normally need to suppress.

Have you ever had that moment when you're thinking something and you say, "That's so wrong!" That goes against everything I believe so why am I even considering doing that. Like I have moments like I'm just walking around the house and I think, *It would really be funny if everyone stepped on the dog's tail.* And then I think, *That's terrible.*

It's moments like those that I think about when I'm writing this. Like just those weird twisted thoughts that come out of nowhere and then go away when you realize they are messed up. It's those weird twisted thoughts that come out of nowhere that you would originally dismiss that I try to put in things like this.

I asked him if he thought we all had these "evil" thoughts but repressed them:

I think so. I do that too—but when I'm writing and when I'm thinking about what I want the characters to do next and I'm not sure what I want to have happen next, I try to pay attention to them and grab on to them and I'm, like, "I just thought of six things that I would not normally say out loud but they'll fit in the situation perfectly."

I have to pay attention to the weird things that I normally wouldn't say and put them in there. Like when a teacher's talking to you really seriously about something, maybe you did something wrong, and you think, *Wouldn't it be fun if I just cracked some random obnoxious joke right now?* But you don't do it. You say, "No, that would definitely not help my situation." But when you're writing it won't help or hurt your situation because it's not you, it's your character.

I suspect that we all have an ambivalent feeling and these transgressive thoughts—they are part of our nature, unavoidable, yet uncomfortable to admit.

At a recent writing conference, I attended a session given by several prominent authors on the question of writing "dark." The speakers agreed that one problem with their students was pulling back from the evil in the story, or the potential evil—in effect, they weren't dark enough. The barrier they identified was the young writers' fear of being identified with a dark character, that if the writers could imagine it, then in some way they *were* that character. They condoned the action, and that undermined their image of being a good person. It's the same thing Ernest said about Stephen King: "He doesn't think, *I wonder if the reader is going to think this is too far, too offensive.* He thinks, *This is how the story is supposed to happen.*"

Similarly, Josie noted that there can be a tendency—which must be resisted—to be too loyal to a main character:

> They have to be completely imperfect, and when you're writing it, it's hard not to want all their decisions to be perfect and right. You have to create them to be realistic. You have to let them make terrible decisions. You have to let them make a decision that is right in the moment and will lead to catastrophic failure in the future. You have to just let that happen. And they need to be true to the story.

And she adds, "They don't need to be brave." She echoes a basic truth of fiction writing, put succinctly by novelist Janet Burroway: "In literature only trouble is interesting. It takes trouble to turn the great themes of life into a story: birth, love, sex, work, and death."

Extensions of the Self

It took some doing to set up my interview with high school senior Macy, an avid fiction writer and student of one of my former students. I had to have a background check, and for the first time in my life was fingerprinted. Once I got word from the state that I had passed, I set up the interview in a local high school. The school entrance, like many in the post–Columbine era, felt more like the waiting area of a minimum-security prison. But once I was buzzed in, I met someone eager to talk about fiction writing

She had shared with me her story "The Room," about a girl in counseling, which begins:

> His voice brings back memories of dark rooms and broken bones. Two months of agony and insanity. Doctor Alan Monroe cannot let my tragic experience go, even though I have.

I asked her to read aloud a paragraph I had chosen, describing the silent tension between this girl and her therapist:

We continue to stare at each other, as we always do during these sessions. Our eyes do the speaking for us, screaming with only our gazes. The room may be silent, but we're not. Tension hangs above us, a string pulled too tight. My senses have heightened since my disappearance, so I can feel when it breaks. He wants to speak when I do not. Our dancing eyes snap away from each other, just as the string breaks in two, curling up on either side of the room. He clears his throat and tries to break our continued silence.

I commented that I loved the image of the string snapping and curling.

Over her high school years her writing had shifted from what she called "high fantasy" to more realistic and dark fiction. I asked her about the satisfaction she got from "going dark."

Relief. I feel a lot of relief from going there and I don't know why. After I write it down, I feel a lot better. I'm, like, "Do I feel something I don't know about?" I've written a lot of dark stuff and maybe there is some part of me that I don't know about and I want to discover that.

I asked her to take me inside her head:

Macy: I think too much about their story that I feel like it's happening to me. I feel so attached to these characters and their stories that I can actually feel their emotion.

TN: Even though it's never happened to you?

Macy: Yeah, even though it's never happened, I feel like it's happened. It's that intense for me. I feel it's happened to me and it hasn't, and it's hard to come back from that. It hasn't happened, but what if it did and I don't remember it. Yeah, an alternate reality, but real.

I like that out-of-body experience, I guess you could call it. It's not who I am but I can imagine it as me. I can see this happening—hopefully it wouldn't happen but I can imagine it and I can see myself in the position.

By writing this intensely she feels that she expands her own capacity for empathy and her personal resilience. She admits that her own life is in the "low distress" end of the spectrum, but there are advantages of imagining more distressful lives:

> We're on the low distress side, but I'm satisfied because I know what the feeling is like. So if I had to experience it, I would have some prior knowledge—if something horrible would happen I'd be able to feel it—and not freak out, like I'd be able to somehow calmly approach this because I'd already felt it.
>
> I'd be able to expand beyond what I already feel and I think that's important for any writer or any person—to put themselves in someone else's shoes and feel what someone else would feel.

For me, the most intriguing line of this interview was "maybe there is some part of me that I don't know about and I want to discover that." It recalls something another of my interviewees said: "Sometimes you don't want to get stuck on this plane of existence."

While Macy doesn't use the term *alter ego* she seems to suggest that something more than empathy for others is going on. She seems to suggest that there is a different "plane of existence," an alternate reality in which she has within herself experiences and emotions, not accessible in "normal" life. This idea of multiple selves became popular in the nineteenth century when hypnotist Anton Mesmer brought out different personalities of individuals under hypnosis (hence the term *mesmerize*). It is celebrated in Robert Louis Stevenson's *The Strange Case of Dr. Jekyll and Mr. Hyde* and Joseph Conrad's *The Secret Sharer.*

In the 1970s this concept was given life in the biography of Sybil Dorsett (Schreiber 1973), who was thought to have sixteen different personalities. This multiplicity was a huge disability for Sybil, but for many of the teenage girls who read it (my daughter included) or watched the TV series with Joanne Woodward and Sally Fields, there was an attraction to imagining that there is more to us than the one "normal" personality.

Tomasen Carey invited her Writers Academy students to explore alternate selves, first by inviting them to choose a different name (using an excerpt from *The House on Mango Street* as a prompt).

> *The next day we picked up from there and asked students to consider their alter ego. Who are they or would they be if they had a different name? The joy and delight as each writer created someone they wished they could be was palpable.*

The most dramatic was the "perfect" female student we had come to love in just two short days! She was animated, bubbly, funny, and eager to participate. She was a leader, bringing new friends into her group and extending herself to the class as a whole. She was "it." She had her role as student down to a tee and she appeared to revel in it. Or did she? We thought so until she revealed her alter ego where she named herself Blue.

We developed these alter egos in terms of their likes, dislikes, places in the world, etc. We then had dress-up stuff available for them to come to the Academy the next day dressed as their alter egos and yes, that included us, the instructors. Blue came in with blue hair, blue lipstick, and every stitch of blue clothing she owned. Her demeanor changed as she was broody, flip, and downright rude even. It honestly stopped me in my teaching tracks.

Who was this girl really and how much pressure must she be under to constantly perform as that perfect student? How completely she embodied her alter ego and let her guard down, to be Blue. To be less than perfect.

In her short sketch "Self-Care of a Mad Man," eleventh grader Caroline takes one of her personality traits—her disorderliness—and inverts it to describe a "mad man," addicted to precise routines, indeed someone we might describe as obsessive-compulsive or even agoraphobic. Here is how it begins:

He came out of his mildewed shower feeling like a new man. He wrapped a red towel around his waist. He ran a thin-toothed comb through his black hair that he slicked back on Mondays and Thursdays. He grabbed his toothbrush with an aggressive fist. He flossed every day . . .

The mold between the tiles has been there since he moved in and will be there until the day he dies. Which he presumes will be soon.

He spits out his toothpaste. Always one string of drool hanging from the left corner of his mouth. He grabs the box of floss he buys every Sunday at the grocery store along with: bread, cheese, ham, mayonnaise and Irish whiskey if he is feeling up for it or if he has company coming over. That doesn't happen very much though. He doesn't like company. And company doesn't seem to like him much either.

Caroline patiently details this man's obsessive, habit-driven process of dressing:

> He walked over to his brown five drawer dresser. From top to bottom it goes: socks and underwear, shirts, pants, pajamas, and an assortment of ties, bowties, and one pair of swim trunks. He put on a pair of white and blue underwear. He took showers only in the morning, at night it felt wrong. Like chaos was about to ensue.

She concludes with him putting on his brown loafers and walking "out the door to the chaos world." She inhabits, with great skill and detail, the psychological state of a depressed, reclusive man, an alter ego, if you will.

Eva's story "Cherry Soda Dreams" is similarly an act of emotional extension. It begins with a vivid depiction of the monotonous unpleasantness of spending time in a sketchy laundromat, drinking warm soda, waiting:

> She rested with one leg beneath her body while the other bounced restlessly on the pale porcelain floor tiles. The fizz of her cherry soda invaded her senses as she brought the bottle to her pink, chapped lips, gulping down a sip of the now room temperature drink. The sweet sugar taste momentarily muffled her senses and blocked out the monotonous flipping and whirling of the laundry machines as the burning summer sun beat down on her back. It seeped through the cobwebbed windows and went on to glare off of the metal walls and clear circle windows of the dizzy machines. The golden rays highlighted each particle of dust and lint which hung in the air. She shifted, pulling her legs to rest sideways on the blue plastic chair sporting a mess of scratches and a strip of black duct tape.

The story was inspired by a photo she took in a local laundromat, at the end of the day—the interior was dim, the fluorescent lights flickering—in her words, "gross." The main character is lonely and longing for the return of her brother, who is deployed overseas.

> I tend to write a lot about not necessarily personal experience but what a personal experience would be like. For "Cherry Soda Dreams" it's about a girl who dreams about her brother coming back from the military. My dad was in the military for twenty-four years and my brother is joining the military so it is

what I would imagine it would be like but also what it was like when my dad came back from deployment.

I asked her about what it is like to write about emotions she has not specifically felt:

I wrote a poem about heartbreak. I've never felt that physically—what the poem was alluding to. But it doesn't really matter what emotion it is. I kind of make it up or imagine what it would be based on what I've experienced before.

Writing about emotions I've never had doesn't limit me at all. I'm free to imagine it any way I want. Where if I felt the emotion before I know exactly what it feels like and I can't expand on it more than what I know. But if I am writing about heartbreak I'm imagining what I would feel based on texts that I have read—and obviously authors have different styles so I'm incorporating feelings I get from different books and making it my own combination.

In the story, weeks went by following this dreary routine, but one evening she is in her apartment and the doorbell ("that she wasn't aware still worked") sounded. Her brother enters her apartment and greets her.

His mouth hung open to say the first words and they met her ears as if she had never been able to hear before this moment.

Tomasen Carey uses a set of props and costumes to create what she calls a "path" to imagining another self—we would see her carting around a big box with ornate hats, scarves, and random objects like shoes or musical instruments or kitchen utensils.

They get this costume which doesn't make sense—and some kind of object. And I tell them the object is the problem. It can be anything from a spoon to a shoe, but it gives you a path. If you give them a problem you can think about what you're wearing and make it go from there. It's silly. There are no high stakes. It's like, be as goofy as you can be and see where we can make it go. The hat and the thing. And then there's extra stuff—scarves. But the hat and the thing. The hat is what you become and the thing is your problem.

It was kind of a running joke that whenever Tomasen brought out her big box, I disappeared—until one day I was cornered. I put on an ornate hat with feathers, wrapped a boa around my neck, and was handed a ukulele. My problem was—why would a woman dressed in this finery have a ukulele?

I imagined her as a widow, and the ukulele was her husband's, and it brought back memories of the times he played in a jug band in college when they met, and of a particular song that was the band's theme song—"The Eggplant That Ate Chicago."

The hat and the thing—it worked for me.

Two Stories of Personal Growth

For eighth grader Caitlyn fiction writing allows her not so much to create an alter ego but a character embodying themes and desires and intensified emotions drawn from her own life. She is an only child who—in her fiction—constantly imagines herself in the role of caretaker for young children and animals. She is, by her own admission, subject to anxiety, and in her stories she returns to situations, where, through momentary inattention, a child or pet is lost, and the main character panics and descends into self-accusation. In fact, she mentioned a story she had written in fifth grade about a lost dog, so she had been circling around this theme for at least four years. In her story "Hunter," she pulls in these recurring identity themes, these strands from her own emotional life, to describe a young girl coping with the loss of her father.

The plot of "Hunter" focuses on the main character, Avery, who has suffered from, and is in some denial about, the death of her father from pancreatic cancer four years earlier.

> It's like the father is always in the story. He never leaves the story.

In a flashback she recalls him teasing her about boyfriends—and the cheesy anniversary cards her parents would send each other, and their embarrassing shows of affection. She also recalls their one last camping trip to the woods behind her house when the cancer was well advanced. Reentering these woods was an act of bravery on Avery's part, an attempt to come to terms with the loss, and at first there seems a kind of reassurance:

> I had been afraid for so long to be reminded of my father, and
> now, in the midst of these trees I feel as if he is standing next to
> me. The trees surround me, and as I exhale I feel overwhelmed.

Early in the story there is almost an equivalence, the forest as a stand-in for her father, both supporting her and standing by her. But this comforting mood is shattered when her dog runs off during this moment of release, as if she can't get away from "loss."

Her first reaction is sheer panic, a state she has described in her other stories, and has experienced herself:

> I scream Hunter's name, until the tears dry up and my voice
> goes hoarse. After looking for an hour I start to panic more. I
> scream out loud, "Idiot, you're such an idiot!" I put my hands to
> my eyes, and I fall to my knees. I feel like I can't breathe. I feel
> my heart pounding in my chest, and there is an awful ache in
> my stomach, like someone punched me. My breathing is getting
> faster, and I sound out of control. . . .

She realizes that she is so overcome with panic that she seems to have given up on really finding her dog. She works to control her breathing—and lies on her back.

> I lay on the moss, in the calming woods, numb. I am past
> sadness. I miss my dad. He is the entire reason I came here
> in the first place. I need my father. Who is there to give me a
> hard time about my boyfriends? Tease me? Support me like no
> other man on earth. No one. Because that man has died. He has
> left the place I live. He has left, and suddenly, it has actually,
> completely hit me, that I will never get him back.

"I lay on the moss, in the calming woods, numb." The woods are no longer the surrounding comfort, no longer "calming." They make vivid her loss—and she keeps repeating the fact that he is gone—and now she suffers a double loss, her father and her beloved dog, who also has associations with the father.

She wakes out of this sad reflection and hears yelling, which she thinks might have something to do with Hunter, and she comes upon a big house where a "strange elderly woman" has the dog and is handling him roughly. Avery demands that she give the dog back, but the woman grabs her by the wrist and begins dragging both of them into the house—forcing her into an act of physical bravery:

> I give her a judging look, and when she sees, she tightens her grip on my wrist. She drags Hunter and I a few more yards until we reach the stairs. I can tell she is getting tired from dragging the two of us, so when she turns one way to reach the door, I kick blindly. I feel contact with a shin, hear a yelp of pain, and hit the granite stairs. I start sprinting, Hunter is close behind.

They escape, but are still lost in the woods, blindly following paths, but there is the sense that the numbness is gone. She stares at the "quickly brightening sky," and she again lies on the forest floor, this time with Hunter. Soon she hears voices, "I close my eyes ready for my angry mom, but all I hear is 'I love you.'" But she is angry:

> "You could've died out there! What were you thinking?!," my mom yells, her hands flailing in the air.
> "I'm sorry, I just . . ." I trail off staring at a stick near my feet. Suddenly I feel my face getting hot.
> "I MISS DAD OK." I stomp on the stick in anger and hear a satisfying crunch in my burst of temper.

It's an important confrontation:

> Her mom is obviously hurt too—and they're both upset—and they have a lot of built-up emotion—and this is them putting it out.

I asked if this outburst was a good thing:

> Yeah, kind of. It kind of gets that emotion out. Sometimes when I'm upset and I'm like mad I need someone to yell at—and not in a mean way. I don't want to yell at someone and make them sad. I can't let that emotion build up and she let that emotion build up for four years—when she was avoiding the forest—and because of this they're exploding. She's kept it from her mom, not talking about it, and pretending it's all normal.

I asked her if she thought Avery matured because of this experience:

She isn't necessarily more mature. I think she's still hurt about losing her dad, but she's come to accept it and she still has Hunter. In this last bit I didn't necessarily think that Avery just had Hunter back. It's also "I still have a piece of my dad." Because she had Hunter when her dad was alive and she still has Hunter. She still has him with her. She knows her dad is not coming back—but she knows she still can move on and still have a life and it's not going to be miserable for her because she's going to figure it out.

In "Hunter" Caitlyn is able to weave so many of the themes of her emotional and family life: her affection for her own parents, her desire to be the caretaker, the experience of a family member dying of cancer, her affection for nature, for animals, and her insights into denial, loss, grief, anger, and guilt. To use the expression of one of her classmates, she is able to "rope in" so much. She plays on complex emotional associations—father equals nature equals Hunter—and tries to show that one way of coping is to hold on to those associations, even when they call to mind the loss itself. Entering the forest was the initial act of bravery that set in motion other acts of bravery and recovery. That's what Avery was able to "figure out."

Portrait of a Friend

We have met eighth grader Grayson briefly already—he is the one who would put all the planning charts his teachers gave him into the paper shredder. He described how he started his NaNoWriMo novel, *Three Kids, Two Actions, One Life Changed*:

> The story kind of took off. I started writing in Mrs. Bradley's class—and it was quiet, everybody plugged into their music and everybody was just typing. And I kind of went into this zone, and when she stopped us I looked at what I had written and I thought, *That's not what I was going to write*. But I went with it.

Here is how he started:

> My brain is hurting, and I just want to go home. The room is so bright and so loud. I wouldn't be able to sleep if a billion dollars

was on the line. The kids around me are chatting up a storm. My teacher is blasting the "clean up" song. I take a look at the clock. Crud, still can't read time. I'm never going to get out of this miserable place.

In this way, we are introduced to eight-year-old Jeffrey, the main character, and his difficulty with the overstimulation of the room is the effect of his autism. Grayson is basing Jeffrey on one of his own close friends:

I actually adore this kid and he really inspires me—I know that sounds cheesy—but he's, like, pretty amazing to be honest. He's a cancer survivor, he might be cross-diagnosed with autism and Down syndrome. He's learning to read and talk. He's doing things that were never imagined. He's being a normal kid while he's doing that. He's going to school, he's playing with friends on the playground, and it amazes me when I look back at how much progress he's made, and I wanted to capture that in a story. So I changed up some of the stuff and gave it a different twist on his life—but I find it so interesting how people with these setbacks can make the best of it—and bloom from what people thought they could never do.

Jeffrey, as you might imagine, is vulnerable to teasing and bullying—and in the story there are two incidents. In one a classmate, Oscar, is jealous of the attention Jeffrey gets at show-and-tell, and later picks a fight with Jeffrey, only to be saved by Gavin, a character modeled after Grayson:

I don't understand humans to be totally honest. The fact that we can be so mean and aggressive toward others just because they're different from the "normal." It frustrates me—and I wanted to take a hit on that in my story.

A central event in Jeffrey's life was his father's abandonment of the family when he was very young. This phenomenon is fairly common, a father refusing to acknowledge or accept the responsibility of dealing with a disabled or severely ill child. The playwright Arthur Miller famously refused to acknowledge his own child with Down syndrome (Tisch 2018). Jeffrey is haunted by a recurring dream connected to his hospital stay when he was being treated for cancer:

I hear the muffled voices of my parents outside the small room. I am hooked up to all the medical supplies under the sun, and machines beep in a constant rhythm. My bed is small, and I am watching a baseball rerun from the 2010 World Series. The table in the corner is filled with flowers and "You Can Beat It" balloons. My energy level is low, and I am just recovering from the last dose of chemo. I hear my parents' voices raise, and I see their shadows through the tinted glass.

After at least five minutes of arguing, my dad yelled, "He isn't worth the bill anyways."

When he started, Grayson was not planning on this plot twist that created a cloud over the whole story:

> That was not where I was planning to go with my story. But when it came across I thought it was such a good plot twist that would worsen his situation and make the people around him that much more important.
>
> That was Jeffrey's weakness—other than the obvious. And the dream that kept recurring played a big part in who he was and how he dealt with situations. The dream was more than a dream—it was a reality. I don't know how to put it. [*Pause*] He lived it. His father did leave under those circumstances. It was more a recurrence of what had actually happened during that time in his life—and he's just playing it over and over again in his head. It's like a memory that doesn't go away—and it happens when he is sleeping. I don't know where that came from—but when I wrote it I made it a big part of my story.

Grayson made no mention of researching trauma for this story—the idea of this recurring dream just seemed to happen in the writing. But he has accurately described the nightmares that are common in post-traumatic stress disorder: "At least 50% of PTSD patients suffer from re-experiencing nightmares that incorporate clear elements or even exact replications of a traumatic event." These intrusive memories "can be remarkably vivid, overwhelmingly emotional, and are experienced as if they are really happening then and there" (Carr 2016).

As Grayson states, the recurrence of this memory—these flashbacks to abandonment—create the need for support from family, school, and friends. And Jeffrey gets that support. The school does not tolerate the bullying and works hard to be inclusive. His family surrounds him with reassuring and familiar rituals—many of them connected to Disney movies, particularly *Toy Story*, which Jeffrey watches again and again. I asked Grayson if Disney was a character in the story:

> Yeah, you're right. The boy I'm basing this off of—movies and shows are his, like, zen. If he is having a hard day, or if he's off his hinges, he sits down and watches a Disney show and he instantly just calms down. . . . And I wanted Jeffrey to have something like that to enjoy it. Like it's just a safe haven, something he can count on to make him happy.

Grayson's inclusion of Disney in his story reminded me of Ron Suskind's deeply moving account of his own severely autistic son, Owen, who simply closed down at age three. It was through Disney that they got him back, watching repetitively the shows Owen watched, impersonating characters in the movies. It became a family thing (2014).

In a similar fashion, as Grayson's story nears its end, Jeffrey's sister Ava pulls a big box from the closet, a 6,000-piece Lego set with instructions on how to make characters from *Toy Story*:

> After four and a half hours, I take a step back and look at the masterpiece we made. All of this time for a beautiful sculpture of Buzz Lightyear with Woody on his back. It's about a foot tall, and two feet wide. I am so proud of what we created together, and I love spending time like this with Ava.

For all the love he gets, it has been a tough week—his dog, an official comfort dog, is away for training, Jeffrey has been teased, bullied, hospitalized with a seizure. At the end of the story his mother and sister slip a note in his underwear drawer, affirming their love for him, and that he can be the strongest boy on the face of the earth:

> While reading this letter, I got the biggest smile on my face, and I am so happy to have a family like them. I run down the stairs with incredible determination. I corral Mom and Ava to the couch. Then it happens.
> "Thank you," I say.

This ending springs on the reader (or at least this reader) the realization that for all the observations Jeffrey makes (after all, he is the narrator), he has never spoken. Everything we hear from him in the story is either through a machine or sign language. These are the first words he speaks.

> The toughest part about writing this whole entire novel was making it so all of his communication was through a device or sign language. I'd be writing and there would be a quote with Jeffrey talking—and I'm, like, "Nope, nope, nope, that can't be happening." Because it's kind of like autopilot and your brain takes over and you start saying, "Jeffrey said" but no, I can't have that. It ended perfectly, but I had no clue. I never would have imagined at the start that it would end this way.

And it was a perfect ending.

"I Know How You Feel"

In Richard Ford's (2006) story "How Was It to Be Dead?" the main character has to come to terms with the news that the ex-husband of his wife, legally dead for eight years, has recently resurfaced, very much alive. As he gets the news he defies the reader to imagine his reaction:

> I should say straight out: never tell anyone that you know how she or he feels unless you happen to be, just at that second, stabbing yourself with the very same knife in the very same place in the very same heart that she or he is stabbing. Because, if you're not, then you don't know how that person feels. (2006)

Nevertheless, gifted fiction writers like Ford attempt to portray the psychologies of characters in distress, in trouble. His Frank Bascombe is one of the great characters in American literature.

And I would argue that fiction writing gives young writers a space to attempt practical psychology, to ask what if? What's it like? What's it like to be autistic? Sadistic? Homicidal? Mourning the loss of a parent? Trapped in a basement by a deranged parent? To be sure, there are one-dimensional characters, loads of them, but if we read student work carefully, and if we are curious about this writing, we will find unexpected insights.

It is almost automatic to claim that extending our psychological range is a key reason *we read*. But the case for writing is, I believe, even stronger. As usual, Ernest put it best, and I will give him the last word. I asked him if he used his experience in creating characters:

> I take what I haven't experienced and do my best. I try to throw myself into the characters and live through their experiences so I can get a better idea of what's going on with them and with people in the real world, like Mr. Burn. He lives a sucky life—and I feel his emotions because I try to become the character. I'm Mr. Burn, Mom's dead, Dad's an alcoholic.
>
> Instead of drawing on experience, I draw on inexperience.

Language, Violence, and Distress—Beyond Censorship

There is often a reflexive move in schools whenever a problem arises: create a prohibiting rule. Improper dancing—no more dances. Someone gets hurt playing football on the playground—no more football. It is especially tempting to do this with writing. Ban violence and profanity, and the problem is solved.

But, as I have noted earlier, any plot involves conflict, and any conflict creates the conditions for defeat, anger, disappointment, injury, loss, and emotional extremes. So some form of violence—or the threat of violence—is inherent in most storytelling. It is in the books students read, the movies they watch, and the corridors they walk.

I asked my cohort of teachers how they deal with this potential problem—and they were consistent in arguing that the issue is not black and white, solvable by a clear rule. There was no clear line in the sand they could draw. Rather it was a topic for discussion, often specific to a piece of writing, and one that often needed to be addressed one-on-one. As high school teacher Cathy Sosnowski explains, it's a matter of appropriateness, "based on the purpose for the writing":

> As with anything else, violence and profanity are tools. But why are we using them? Question is—are they the right tools?

Erin Vogler expands this principle:

> When it comes to violence and offensive language in student fiction writing, we always approach it from the lenses of value to the story and audience engagement. We talk about why it's there, whether it has to be there, what it adds, and how it helps connect characters and/or elements of the plot. We also talk about intended audience.
>
> As a writing teacher, I see these moments as opportunities to think about problem solving and writerly decision-making . . . where we really dig into rhetorical situation (message, purpose, audience, genre, stance, design), something that is a vital consideration in every type of writing.
> No matter what, it's always about WHY.

If we explore intent, I suspect that most of these writers are not really glorying violence—they are after suspense, more the *anticipation* of violence, danger. I also feel there is an economy to violence, when it is done well, with a great deal left to the imagination of the reader. Good mentor texts can make this clear. Similarly, profanity can be used to suggest character and emotion, but, like violence, it loses its effectiveness if overused. In other words, the teachers I interviewed treated the issue as a practical one (Does this work in the story? Does it work for the intended audience?) rather than a moral one.

There is, however, one ethical rule that follows from the basic code of school behavior—the need to respect the feelings and well-being of other students. There is no place for writing that embarrasses, threatens, or belittles classmates or teachers. Period. This is not writing about violence; this is violence, itself.

A related anxiety is that in fiction students might reveal emotional trauma, depression, even suicidal thoughts, that puts us in the difficult situation of having to direct them to counseling, possibly disrupting any confidential relationship we might have with them. (To be fair, these revelations can occur in any kind of writing. Even research writing.) Liz Juster's students deal with this by alerting her up front:

> When my students write fiction that includes violence in terms
> of setting or scene, they usually take great pains to make sure
> they seek permission first. They don't want me to misinterpret
> their work as a veiled cry for help or some sort of signal that
> they are premeditating a violent act.

Middle school teacher David Rockower speculates that teachers may be primed to overreact to themes of violence and emotional distress:

> We are trained to consider all these potentially harmful reasons
> that students may write this way, when in reality they are (most
> in my opinion) exploring what it's like to be grown up. Just as
> students read dark dystopian novels with plenty of violence,
> they like to experiment with style and test out the waters of
> living in those worlds from a writer's perspective.

In general, he notes, "When students share their work with others, the adults are more shocked than the students. It seems that most students are not as easily disturbed by violent imagery." When writing becomes excessive he usually works one-on-one to show them that "too much of anything can turn off a reader."

Going back to my own research with young male writers, I have often felt that we get the causal arrows wrong. The logic of prohibiting these dark themes seems to assume that the writing *creates*, in some way, that darkness in the writer—and makes the writer more prone to act in a destructive way. But every survey of wellness in adolescents that I have seen indicates that this darkness is *there*. Anxiety, depression, suicidal ideation *are there* (and becoming more prevalent). A Pew Research Center Survey found that in 2017 one in five teenage girls—or nearly 2.4 million—had experienced at least one major depressive episode in the previous year (Geiger and Davis 2019). Seventy percent of the students interviewed felt depression and anxiety were major problems among their peers. Even those who are not part of these statistics probably have a friend who is. To suppress any writing on this problem does not make it disappear—it only sends the message that this interest is taboo, unwritable, unspeakable. That they must remain alone in experiencing it. What do we gain by this denial?

In Laura LaVallee's senior memoir course, these topics are unavoidable. She is careful that students give trigger warnings if they are dealing with trauma that might be deeply upsetting to some students. She is scrupulous in adhering to legal requirements to report abuse and trauma, though in her school counselors are usually aware of issues. And when they are not, her first step is to encourage the student to "take agency" and make the contact.

Still, she wants students to tell their stories on their own terms:

> *After perhaps years of feeling ashamed of their truth, whether it's an eating disorder or struggling with depression or living with an alcoholic parent, I don't feel like it's my place to tell them how they can or cannot tell their story. Now that they are ready to write and share their story, I don't want them to hold back. I want them to tell it how they want to tell it. It's their decision as a writer coming to terms with their reality on what details to include, not mine.*
>
> *As teachers of writing, we can't expect students to write eloquently about trauma because there is nothing eloquent about it. It's messy and confusing and often really raw, so it's okay if they write about it in the exact same way. Maybe one day when there is enough distance and time for reflection the scene may look very different, but for right now, the act of getting the story just down is good enough. I think my students are incredibly brave.*

She adds, "I was never given the opportunity to be vulnerable in my writing until college and that makes me angry."

6

Going Short

Four Invitations

A good short-short is short but not small, light but not slight.

—Ku Ling, Taiwanese writer

One obvious obstacle to bringing fiction into the curriculum is its unwieldi-ness. There is the ever-present pressure of time. As my friend Tim Dewar has said, "As teachers our currency is our time and we are really poor." It's hard to find a place (not to mention time) to read the sprawling epics many students, like Ernest, want to write. We'll deal with that challenge in the next chapter. But in this one we will deal with shorter, often improvisational op-portunities that can be dropped into our classes at just about any point—they don't need to be a unit. They can be playful, ungraded, unrevised, light. This I *have* attempted in my teaching career, and I will dip into some of my own prompts and how my students (and I) responded.

It started when I came across Jerome Stern's anthology *Micro Fiction: An Anthology of Fifty Really Short Stories* (1996). I'd, of course, heard about flash fiction and other short forms, but as I read through this collection, I was stunned by what skilled writers could do on only a single page. In one selec-tion, the entire story was one long sentence.

I decided to give this big-sentence idea a try in a class of prospective teachers, and the writing seemed to have an intensity of attention that was missing from the more typical assignments I had given. One student, an EMT assistant, wrote such a memorable account of a near-tragic ambulance run that for years I used her piece as a mentor text. She takes the reader so authentically into the mind of an EMT: bored about what seems a routine trip where a young woman had probably taken some pills (probably a few Advils) after a breakup, only to discover later in the day that this woman had a bottle of Percocet, and the woman came close to dying. Clearly Emily came to my class with skills I never taught her, but I also feel that the assignment itself provoked her to experiment with sentence options—asides, all kinds of embedding and elaboration for which she (and even I) don't have names.

When we write the big-sentence assignment, I remind students to use whatever tools they want (parentheses, modifiers, dashes, semicolons, even *and*s) to keep it going. And to try for about a page, 200–250 words. The key is to pick or imagine an experience that is rich in detail and intensity.

Please excuse the inclusion of the photograph in Figure 6–1, but it has a bearing on the sentence I wrote. Several years ago I won a campuswide award, and a photographer contacted me about a shoot. Not in your office, he said, that's too generic.

It was summer, and every noon I swam at the majestic UNH outdoor pool—so I suggested that location, and he agreed. When I mentioned this choice to my family, they weren't so sure ("Dad in a Speedo?"). I assured them that I would not embarrass them—and it turned out to be, in my view, the best photo ever taken of me.

At any rate, a poster was made of this photo and for a few years after the award it was

Figure 6–1 Unconventional author photo

hung in the department lounge, where our biweekly meetings were held. Every time I walked in, it was staring down at me. The following (with some fictionalizing) is what I experienced every department meeting—with this other Tom staring down at me.

It was only ten minutes into the department meeting, but already Tom could feel his mind roaming, as he lost track of the blah, blah, blah about the exact working to the new requirement, blah, blah, blah, and how the word *text* was too restrictive—all which made him feel like he was in elementary school again, bored out of his mind, his mind actually leaving his body to places he'd rather be like the outdoor swimming pool, which was slowly draining on this September day, but there was this absurd picture of him in this same outdoor pool, actually displayed in this very room, for some award he'd won, and Tom felt himself confronted by this other Tom, in a better place, standing at the end of the swimming lane, his Speedo tastefully under the water, which was so perfectly unruffled— the bottom lane lines clearly visible, so inviting, but Tom knew that he was only 10, maybe 11 now, minutes into this meeting and that he should at least pretend to pay attention to his colleagues, who, for all he knew, were also pretending to pay attention, but why didn't someone tell him earlier that such a big part of being an adult was pretending to care about things you could care less about like whether "text" was or was not too restrictive.

Dedicated to all teachers whose minds drift during staff meetings.

Flash Fiction

Stories can obviously be of any length, from the six-word biographies to the epic novels that Ernest created. But it seemed to me that the midrange story of about two to three thousand words was hard for students to manage. Often writers would bring in so many characters and set up such complex plots that they couldn't manage to finish, or they would end their stories abruptly. Finishing, in fact, was a problem many of them identified—it bothered some and was OK with others. But as stories became longer, there was also a problem for teachers—the sheer act of reading lengthy pieces was overwhelming, let alone offering suggestions and keeping track of revisions. It bothered some, and was OK with others, for whom the sheer productivity of the longer piece was a major goal.

Linda Rief, a teacher in our school system (and author of the classic book for teachers, *Seeking Diversity* [1991]), is one of those who find the longer fictional stories unwieldy for teaching craft. Like her counterpart Nancie Atwell, in Boothbay, Maine, she found flash fiction to be an attractive and manageable form for teaching techniques of fiction writing—the very brevity necessitates important choices. Rief explained it this way when I spoke with her:

> *Flash fiction has the characteristics of the short fictional story— what's different is every word has to count. If you're only going to write 750 words you have to make every detail you include in the story be some clue to what is going on. In flash fiction, in particular, it does a 180 degree turn at the very end. So you're reading the story, truly believing what's going on—and in one or two sentences you are totally turned upside down, but you realize it's been so tightly crafted that you almost should have suspected this before you got to those one or two sentences.*
>
> *I just like the tightness of it. I like the fact that the title has to give you the hint about what is happening and what is going to happen. You don't have to spend page after page developing a character. It's almost a snapshot of a character, a snapshot of a scene. The tight crafting of it makes you work really hard—no wasted language.*

She approaches flash fiction like any other genre she introduces to her eighth graders—bottom up, inductively. She finds seven to eight appealing and appropriate mentor texts (including those of former students) and asks, "What do you notice?" The "rules" are derived from the study of mentor texts. Students notice:

- The turn in the story at the end, the surprise.
- The writer jumps right in, no time spent in "getting there." The tension of the plot is established early.
- The title needs to give some clue to what is happening.

- There is one scene—staying in one spot.
- Dialogue needs to be economical, revealing character.
- There are one or two characters.

One of her student mentor texts that she used was called "Diplomacy." It opens with a deliberation in the United Nations where countries agree on nuclear disarmament, including the United States, which placed its 7,000 warheads in a disposal pit in New Mexico—all the other countries similarly deactivated their warheads and sent them to the United States for disposal. "Within months, the world was nuclear free." The story then shifts abruptly to a series of conversations:

> "Are you sure there are no missiles remaining, general?"
> "Yes, our spies are certain, sir. No evidence of remaining missiles."
> "Good. Arm all remaining missiles and launch."
>
> "Generalissimo, are we certain there are no remaining missiles?"
> "Confirmed, no warheads remaining."
> "Good. Arm all remaining warheads and launch."
>
> "Commander, am I correct in assuming all countries have removed their nuclear arsenals?"
> "Correct sir."
> "Good. Arm all remaining warheads and launch." (Evan)

The title of the piece, "Diplomacy," is well-chosen, ironic.

There are many variations—and varying lengths—for this short fiction. One that I encountered recently is the 100-word story, or century. It's a genre close to the prose poem and kissing cousin to the joke, often leading to a punch line. Here is one of my favorites from the collection *Nothing Short Of: Selected Tales from 100 Word Story* (Faulkner, Mundell, and Olson 2018):

"SIDESHOW" BY THAISA FRANK

The sideshow's latest attraction is Brad, a darkly handsome electrician, and his chocolate poodle Rex. They sleep in a featherbed and snore in perfect rhythm. Last summer Brad's wife kicked him out because of his snoring and Brad's grief was so immense that it inspired Rex to synchronize his snores. It was only a matter of time before a talent scout heard them through an open window and the show was packed. Sometimes Brad's ex-wife sneaks in. She trembles with the brilliant thunder of each snore, ignores the rapt, adoring women. *I heard this first,* she whispers to the popcorn-scented dark. (13)

The book's editors claim that writing these centuries teaches concision and immediacy: "They're a flicker of light in the darkness, a pinprick, a thunderclap" (iv).

In her epic third edition of *In the Middle*, Nancie Atwell chronicles her own evolution toward short fiction, detailing difficulties and limitations of long fiction and her earlier requirement that it be strictly realistic—in her words, "everyday."

My students invent people, places, and scenarios. They draw on their voluminous experiences as readers of all kinds of stories as well as the vicarious knowledge they acquire along the way. They tap skills as poets to compress events, select diction, create imagery, suggest themes, and craft killer titles and end lines. (2015, 487)

Paradoxically, by limiting length, she *opened up* the range of what students could do.

Fan Fiction as Literary Criticism

Ninth grader Josie began her own novel as a kind of protest against the way the directors of the TV series *The Hundred* ended season 5:

They majorly screwed up the plot and the characters in my opinion and it didn't feel true to who they were. So you know, "I'm going to finish the season for you."

And so, she joins the great subculture of fan fiction, posting her revised version of *The Hundred* on the mega website Wattpad. This subculture has its own vocabulary (*slash*; *fem slash*; *shipping*; *het*; *AU* [alternative universe]), several popular platforms for sharing, and literally infinite possibilities for altering, and recombining, elements of popular movies, books, TV series, and video games (Romano 2016).

It occurred to me that when Josie says the ending of *The Hundred* was "majorly screwed up," not "true" to the way the plot and characters have evolved in the series, she was performing an act of literary criticism. And that the attraction of fan fiction, or at least one of them, is operating from a deep understanding of characters, to the point where you can imagine them in other settings, and in other relationships. It also occurred to me that we can poach this technique to enhance the reading of novels in class—bridging the divide between creative writing and literary analysis.

Here is how it can work.

In any novel there is a scene or part of the story that is implied but not told—there is a backstory, there are imaginary sequels, what happens after the novel is done. For example, in the 2013 Baz Luhrmann film version of F. Scott Fitzgerald's *The Great Gatsby* we start with Nick Carraway in a psychiatric hospital, recovering from the events of the story. There are also scenes that we get glimpses of in the novel, which a screenwriter might have to expand on.

One such scene takes place after a catastrophic day in New York, with the excruciating confrontation between Daisy and Tom in the sweltering hotel room and the accident on the way back that kills Tom's mistress, Myrtle Wilson. At the end of the day, Gatsby has positioned himself outside the Buchanan mansion, essentially stalking Daisy, where he surprised Carraway. Gatsby asks him to go up to the kitchen window and see if Daisy is all right. Here is Carraway's account:

> Daisy and Tom were sitting opposite each other at the kitchen table with a plate of cold fried chicken between them and two bottles of ale. He was talking intently across the table at her and in his earnestness his hand had fallen upon and covered her own. Once in a while she looked up at him and nodded in agreement.
>
> They weren't happy, and neither of them had touched the chicken or the ale—and yet they weren't unhappy either. There was an unmistakable air of natural intimacy about the picture and anybody would have said they were conspiring together. (1995, 152–53)

We are left to infer what was said—because Carraway can't hear the conversation. But what was said? Did Daisy admit that she was driving the car that killed Myrtle Wilson? How does she explain the fact that Gatsby was sure she would leave Tom for him? What is she agreeing to? And why is she agreeing?

To answer any of these questions, the screenwriter–student needs a sense of this relationship—and writing the missing dialogue is an act of character analysis. How do these deeply flawed characters handle this difficult moment? My friend Marty Brandt posed this challenge to his seniors—and began by inventing a letter, dated July 5, 1924, that Fitzgerald's editor, the legendary Maxwell Perkins, might have sent to Fitzgerald and that ends with a request:

> Finally, there is one scene in the book that bothers me. It's the one after the accident that kills Myrtle, where Nick observes Daisy and Tom "conspiring together." I found myself wanting to know what they're saying. I suggest that you revise that scene: as you establish its setting, make sure the window's open—it's a hot night, after all—add a few lines of dialogue (up to a dozen, at the most), and then share Nick's response to it.
>
> Give my love to Zelda and stay clear of Ernest. He doesn't have your best interest at heart.

Here is his assignment: For your final, you are to rewrite the scene as if you were F. Scott Fitzgerald (Figure 6–2). Make sure to do the following:

- Establish the setting, making use of Fitzgerald's writing style.

- Include six to twelve lines of dialogue between Tom and Daisy, making sure to show your understanding of the characters.

- Finish with Nick's response (again, writing in Fitzgerald's style) in which he shares with his readers the judgments that he would ordinarily keep to himself.

Figure 6–2 F. Scott Fitzgerald

He shared with me the work of one of his students who fully embraced this assignment (writing six pages!). It is hardly typical or representative—but it does show the upper limits of what can happen. Here are two paragraphs:

> "After all," he laughed, and the sound was bitter and confident and humorless to my ear, "That man has nothing on me, don't you think Daisy?" He gave her no time to respond smirking away as he cocked his head to the side in thought. "Thinking he could come and whisk you away after all we've been through, from Chicago to Kapiolani. And he thought he could pull the blinds on everyone—well not this guy!"
>
> Quickly, my eyes widened at the smugness of his words. It felt intrusive to listen to this private conversation between the two, stuck in a corner trying to peer through a small window. I felt ashamed and a little guilty, and yet I hesitated to step away from the window. I felt like I was in a soap opera, albeit a poorly done one with characters I couldn't give sympathy to, and it felt it was my service to keep watching.

Marty commented "Ha!" by this last sentence that so wonderfully captures Nick's conflicted feelings of disdain and fascination—and his need to be of "service" to Gatsby.

In her commentary, Bonnie described her approach to writing this excerpt:

> I know you said, "Your dialogue should accurately portray the concerns that they would have and your understanding of the kind of people they are," but to be honest, I feel that it would be in character for the two to try and pretend that things were OK. Constantly hiding things from each other even murder or scandals—they've done it before (maybe to a lesser extent) and I think they'd definitely do it even if both of them knew the truth.

And she added as a postscript, "I enjoy how Fitzgerald subtly gives a lot of meanings that aren't outright said and I had fun playing and replicating that." This is undeniably close reading, analysis merged with the option to write fiction.

Another obvious opening is to shift point of view, which has often been an opportunity to give voice to silenced or seemingly "minor" characters, often women. A powerful example is Sena Jeter Naslund's *Ahab's Wife: Or, The Star-Gazer*. Cathy Sosnowski would invite her students to take the point of view of Holden Caulfield's psychiatrist (What notes would he write?) or that of Holden's beloved sister, Phoebe (if she wrote a letter to Dear Abby, and Abby's response).

Fiction as Improvisation

In the mid-1970s the great literacy scholar James Britton and his colleagues created some controversy when they linked reading literature with gossip. Gossip, after all, invites evaluation of behavior:

> In telling the tale, the speaker offers (both in what he selects and the way he recounts it) his evaluation of the events narrated and invites in return the evaluation of his listeners. (Britton et al. 1975, 80)

This testing out of value systems offers both speaker and listener a basic social satisfaction. For some this was a demeaning, disrespectful, and inappropriate equation. But I felt it made great sense. After all, when we gossip, we are evaluating human behavior, assigning a name (actually an adjective) to it. Was that remark *rude*? Is she being *foolish*? Have you ever seen someone so *narcissistic*?

It may be the most essential "reading" we do. Indeed, the inability to read human cues is a serious disability associated with autism. A colleague of mine claims that these terms, these adjectives, are the most important vocabulary we possess—since they allow us to interpret social relationships. Similarly, a basic pleasure of reading literature is the activation—and refinement—of judgment. Take the opening paragraphs of Elizabeth Strout's short story "Motherless Child" in which she brings back her legendary character Olive Kitteridge:

> They were late.
> Olive hated people who were late. A little after lunchtime, they had said, and Olive had the lunch things out, peanut butter and jelly for the two oldest kids, and tuna-fish sandwiches for her son, Christopher, and his wife, Ann. For the little ones, she had no idea. The baby was only six weeks old and wouldn't be eating anything solid yet; little Henry was over two, but what did two-year-olds eat? Olive couldn't remember what Christopher had eaten when he was that age. (2019, 57)

So what do we make of Olive? Which adjective would we apply? Possibly *judgmental* or *inflexible*—she seems unable to adjust to the late arrival of her son and his family, not an uncommon circumstance when people are travelling a distance. But I would pick *anxious*, almost *panicked* about the food for the kids (and we may infer about the visit itself). This form of close reading, to use the popular term, is simply an extension of our social, gossip-grounded, capacity to read behavior—endlessly interesting.

Eighth grader Nazia asks something similar of us when she introduces Deborah Smith "the most basic debate mom in all of California," who lives in an affluent suburb of Los Angeles and who is known to "go off at the judges when her kid loses. Which is most of the time." Nazia's narrator and main character, Jamilah, gives Ms. Smith a "plastic smile," after she bests Ms. Smith's son in a debate contest. Jamilah "consoles" her:

> "Yeah, this year all the kids are working so hard—even if
> they aren't winning. I think that's so *brave* of them, right?"
> I draw out the last couple of words and see Ms. Smith's thin
> lips crumple up into a frown. I know it is sort of rude, but with
> the number of times she's called me out in front of judges for
> winning, she deserves it.

A number of adjectives come to mind, other than *rude*—*clever, defiant, assertive*—clearly a narrator I want to stay with as a reader.

This capacity to reveal character through behavior is a primary skill of the fiction writer—it invites the reader to continually infer, interpret, and pass judgment. The classic "show, don't tell." In my own first-year college writing class, I wanted my students to explore this process, first through dramatic improvisation, then writing.

I started simply. I owned a fish tie, which when knotted around my neck made it appear as if a trout was suspended from my neck, a Christmas present from one of my kids. In class, I took off my regular tie, and put on the fish tie. "What would you think," I asked, "if I came into class the first day looking like this?"

There was a pause, and a student answered, "Well, I'd think you had a sense of humor."

Another followed. "Sure, you had a sense of humor, but I'm not sure I would like the sense of humor."

A third said it would remind her of the silly ties that her elementary school principal wore.

We moved from these demonstrations to short, charade-like skits. I gave students a set of situations in which character traits might be revealed—the most popular being "to engage a reluctant fellow passenger in a conversation." Easily the most dramatic occurred when Bean (that's what he went by), fresh from boot camp, circled menacingly around his partner, Andrew:

> **Bean:** *Give me five, Soldier.* (Andrew drops to push-up position.) *What are you doing down there, Soldier? That wasn't me, that was someone else. Need to get your ears cleaned. Get up.* (Bean closes in to within six inches of his face.) *What do you take me for, Soldier, stupid?*
>
> **Andrew:** *No, sir.*
>
> **Bean:** *I didn't hear you, Soldier.*
>
> **Andrew** (*Louder*): *No, sir.*
>
> **Bean:** *Give me five, Soldier.*

By the end of the skit, Andrew had done forty-five push-ups!

I explained that fiction writing involved a similar kind of improvisation—getting inside a character and imagining the ways they would talk, act, and think. But before setting up the assignment I wanted students to look at some excerpts of fiction in which characters are revealed through what they do. Fortunately, we had an example written by Andie, a class member, as her response to Irvin Yalom's *Love's Executioner* (2012). Many of Yalom's case studies involved depression, something Andie had seen firsthand. In her story "In Living Color," she imagines a young woman whose mother has gone mad and who is slipping over the edge as well. Andie describes this young woman, on a bridge, leaning forward, imagining her own suicide, her vision becoming blurry.

I took a try at this assignment focusing on a trait I possess—indecisiveness. I am one of those people who, whatever they order in a restaurant, cannot get out of their mind the options they are foregoing. So I wanted to push this trait to an extreme with William, who is paralyzed by choice.

> William got the digital clock in the divorce—he couldn't figure out why. He hated the way it clicked away his life. He hated its precision. Click 6:57. The house, now that Adam and Rob were gone, was so quiet the click could be heard downstairs. He thought about throwing it out but that would be a dramatic gesture and William hated dramatic gestures.

He slowly moved to his clothes closet to choose a tie, walking past his desk where he saw a cup still filled with the dreg of coffee, three or four days old, which had developed a white mold. There were cups like this all over the house and William would take them to the dishwasher soon.

Choosing a tie. He hated choosing ties because he could never figure out the rules. He could figure out one rule—a plain tie on a plain shirt was usually OK except maybe blue on green. But when you came to striped ties and print shirts he was confused. He didn't know the rules. So he would go down the stairs to Rachel and she would nod yes or shake her head no. He admired the ties men were wearing now, the garish, wide-bodied things. But he couldn't see himself wearing one.

The story shifts to a memory of his son Adam, similarly paralyzed when buying a souvenir on Causeway Street after a Boston Red Sox game. Finally, William just buys a Roger Clemens shirt for him—and Adam "sucked on the edges of it all the way home."

William looked at the ties in his closet. A blue one with red stripes, and an old paisley one from the 1970s that had gone in and out of fashion a couple of times. Both would work, he thought. It was as if the balance was so level, the choice so meaningless, that he couldn't make it, couldn't tilt toward either side. He was paralyzed by the pure insignificance of what he was doing.

He looked at the clock, the excessively precise clock, click 7:53. He would be late to the morning meeting. He was sure of it now. The department chair would notice and tuck that bit of information away to be brought out when salaries were decided. William held a tie in each hand, frozen to the spot, and began to cry.

One of my students, Michelle, began with a short sketch of her main character, Mikah, and developed it into a full short story that described her infatuation with a college student, Jim, and his brutal date-rape of her.

In one paragraph she has described the swirl of conflicting emotions— shame, anger, self-disgust, inadequacy, uncleanliness—that a rape victim feels (one of Michelle's goals was to be a rape counselor). She is aware that the victim, though terribly abused, can still shift the blame to herself. It was one of the most memorable pieces of writing I had ever received.

My short foray into fiction writing was not a complete success. Many students picked characters distant from their experience, creating stock characters that—at best—called up stock responses. Some simply didn't know their characters well enough. As always, my direction and planning could have been better, slower. But there were often gems within these sketches, images or descriptions that seemed true and right. Here, for example, is how Andrew (recovered from his push-ups) described Harry, a hard-drinking, rural New Englander whose wife has left him:

> Harry had just finished hauling wood for the day. His back
> ached with pain and his right bicep was bulging with
> pressurized blood from holding the big Johnson chain saw. His
> red and white flannel jacket was coated with chainsaw dust
> and woodchips. He smelled like oil and gas mixed with sweat.

I loved the image of the *pressurized blood*. And sometimes, it is just a single well-chosen word that can redeem a day or week. As when Nazia describes the arrogant helicopter parent, whose son loses the debate—how Jamila's retort causes "Ms. Smith's smile to crumple into a frown." How great is *crumple*?

• •

In my interviews with teachers, one common thread was the importance of writing with students, of being a practitioner of the genres we teach. Not experts, not published authors, but fellow writers. The act of writing gives us insights and experiences that are not available if we view writing instruction as merely a set of procedures—in other words, if we view it from the outside. We must know the experience of writing in our bodies, know the way it feels. D. H. Lawrence called this embodied knowledge "blood consciousness," which he contrasted with "mind consciousness": "We can go wrong in our minds. But what our blood feels and believes and says, is always true" (2000, 53). So when we model, and share our writing and experience of writing, we are cuing students into this inner game of composing.

I asked each of the teachers I interviewed to imagine a highlight reel of their teaching—imagine themselves at their very best. What would be on that reel? This question usually prompted a pause, the intake of breath; it's not a question they usually hear. Eighth-grade teacher Mark Holt-Shannon answered this way:

I think I'm good at modeling. I model when my writing sucks.
I'm writing a story along with them—I promise that it's a new
idea, not something I've done before—a brand-new idea—and
I write with them. And I think one of the things that gets a lot
of kids is my enthusiasm about using writing to dig and dig and
dig and discover something new and say it in a way that sounds
great. I'm in the trenches. I'm doing this too—sometimes it's
hard, and sometimes it pays off if you keep digging.

As he sees it, fiction writing is embedded in a classroom culture that
features oral storytelling:

To teach story you have to tell stories. We tell a lot of stories.
We laugh a lot. There's a connection to the fiction writing
when we're just talking and kind of basking in that feeling of a
well-told story.

The invitations that I have described in this chapter can be low-risk
entry points for writing fiction, playful, and capable of being wedged into a
packed curriculum. They can also be an entry point for teachers like myself
for whom fiction writing seemed a special talent that I did not possess. I
didn't have to commit myself to a long story, or novel, just to a sketch or an
extended sentence, or an invented conversation. I might, for example, just
hand out laminated copies of the great Richard Avedon's photos of the American West. These portraits were taken in front of a white sheet that eliminated
any background and made the people seem so vulnerable. I'd ask students to
tell their stories—Boyd Fortin, a thirteen-year-old rattlesnake skinner, holding a snake and its entrails. What is on his mind? It wasn't full-form fiction,
more what Cathy Sosnowski calls "prefiction," sketches, impressions. Play.

In my own classes, I never felt like I was a model—more a fellow writer.
I would share my writing, invite others to share—and as I think back on my
entire teaching career, I treasure those first minutes of class where we would
just try out a prompt. How often this writing was just better, freer, looser than
that of the papers my students wrote. It was a magical time, not always but
frequently. I kept all my attempts in marble notebooks, dozens of them, and in
looking back I realized how important this in-class writing was *for me*, how I
became a fluent writer and storyteller by writing with my students.

7

Going Long

Writing the Novel

And when it comes to the topsy-turvy world of the
rough draft, the law of the land is best summed
up in two words, exuberant imperfection.

—Chris Baty, *No Plot? No Problem!*

A number of years ago I spent several days in a Hawaiian school as a consultant and speaker. I'd do demonstrations, meet with teachers, and at one point was featured in a middle school assembly where students would ask me questions that they had prepared in their classes.

I should have sensed trouble when I was introduced as a "writer." The questions came.

"Are your stories related to your life?"

"Well, I don't exactly write fictional stories. I write books for teachers."

"How do you figure out your plots?"

"You see, my books don't have plots. They have ideas for teachers."

"How do you create your characters?"

Sigh. "I don't have made-up characters . . ."

I swear I could almost see the thought bubbles forming above the kids' heads: "Why are we here with this loser?" At this point, the embarrassed teacher who had introduced me jumped in, "He's not *that* kind of writer. He writes nonfiction about education."

At the time I chalked this up as just one more weird situation you find yourself in when you go on the road. But as I recall the awkwardness of it, the lesson is this: that for these students a Writer is a fiction writer. A real writer, that is. Other people may do writing, but they are not Writers. The novel is the true test of the Writer. I have found that this view is even shared by accomplished essayists and nonfiction writers—they haven't earned the designation of Writer unless they write a novel.

As I have noted, many young novelists choose to work off the educational grid, on their own terms. Linda Rief compares it to sandlot baseball, no adults hovering, making rules, no umpires, no giving out grades. But the National Novel Writing Month (NaNoWriMo) organization, a national nonprofit supporter of student writing, has brought novel writing into 10,000 classes nationwide (with over 450,000 annual participants, adults included). I spoke with Grant Faulkner, the executive director, who summarized the mission of NaNoWriMo this way:

> *We believe in creativity for creativity's sake, in creativity as an end in itself. Our mission—and what we are good at—is empowering people to believe in their creativity, and helping them get over whatever obstacles that are between them and the story they want to get on the page.*

To accomplish this mission they have created a wealth of supporting materials—a robust website with lesson plans and apps for setting goals and counting words; summer camps; pep talks; and motivational guides such as *No Plot? No Problem! A Low-Stress, High-Velocity Guide to Writing a Novel in 30 Days* (2004) by NaNoWriMo founder Chris Baty. And Faulkner's own co-authored guide (with Rebecca Stern), *Brave the Page: A Young Writer's Guide to Telling Epic Stories* (Stern and Faulkner 2019).

You catch something of the spirit of NaNoWriMo with this workbook advice to middle school students to silence or contain their "inner editor":

> An Inner Editor is the negative, no-fun beast we bring along with us on all our creative endeavors. It sits on our shoulder and points out misspellings and every awkward sentence. When it's in a particularly nasty mood, it tells us we're awful writers and shouldn't be allowed to say anything at all. . . .

> So, no matter how ridiculous this might sound, close your eyes and imagine your Inner Editor. When does it pop up? What does it look like (three-headed dictionary monster breathing red ink fire, perhaps)? What kinds of things does it say?

The workbook then provides an "Inner Editor Containment Button" that the writer is asked to press.

I must admit, I approached my interviews with novel-writing teachers, and students, with a kind of starry-eyed admiration. They all had accomplished something I had never tried. So, I'll organize this chapter around my own questions.

How Do You Launch?

When I interviewed eighth grader Grayson, he noted that all his teachers required him to fill out planning charts before his writing, but if he had his way, he would put all of them in the paper shredder. Planning like this got in the way. Ideas would come to him as he wrote—in his words, he "goes ballistic." Similarly, Adarsh, when asked what advice he would give to teachers, said, "Don't confine them to a certain idea. Let them roam free. If they get a little too out of the box you can tell them and restrict them a bit." Most importantly, he stressed, don't confine them to a "small area." I asked what would be a "small area" that students might be confined to:

> Like you have to have a backstory, you have to have rising action, you have to have a conflict, you have to have falling action, you have to have a resolution. My story goes conflict, falling action, another mini-conflict, falling action, resolution, question mark.

That's pretty much the advice that Chris Baty gives:

> It may seem counterintuitive, but when it comes to novel writing, more preparation does not necessarily produce a better book. In fact, too much preparation has a way of stopping novel writing altogether. As reassuring as it is to embark on your writing journey with a mule-team's worth of character traits, backstories, plot twists, metaphors, and motifs, it's also a 100 percent viable strategy to walk into the wilds of your novel with nothing but a bottle of water and a change of underwear. (2004, 84)

Laura Bradley doesn't require students to pack a mule-team's worth of material but she does ask them to create a plot outline, as bullet points, and to imagine ways in which the novel might end. Other teachers do some version of a storyboard, something as simple as folding a piece of paper several times to create small squares to sequence the action. Storyboarding is, of course, a standard technique to plan movie plots, an appealing connection because the students I talked to often imagine their novels *as movies.*

A key concept for Bradley is the "inciting incident," the problem that sets the plot in motion, and she created a video sequence with images that illustrated the trouble or disruption that launches several popular novels. Among the novels she uses are:

- *Hatchett* by Gary Paulsen. Brian Robeson crash-lands a plane in the northern Canadian wilderness.
- *Harry Potter and the Sorcerer's Stone* by J. K. Rowling. Harry discovers he's a wizard.
- *What Happened to Cass McBride?* by Gail Giles. Kyle Kirby is being interrogated about the disappearance of a popular girl in his school.
- *If I Stay* by Gayle Forman. Mia Hall is in a coma after a car accident.

By the time she is done, the students are primed to start.

Scott Storm, a high school teacher in New York City, begins his novel-writing unit, in his words, by "just being the weird English teacher":

We start, usually on the first day, we move all the furniture to the side—and everyone lies down on their backs on the floor, and I play some instrumental music. Usually I play Johan de Meij's Lord of the Rings Symphony. *I do a kind of imaginative story as they're listening to the music. I tell a story—and it's done in the second person—"You feel like this" "And now you're running" "You're flying." So they're doing these things and they're visually imagining that they're happening. And then we wake up and free-write right away. I do a series of very strange things in order to get people to first be OK in this very collaborative space but also to know that writing can come from a lot of different places.*

I also got advice from students I interviewed. Ninth grader Ethan wrote dark horror stories, but he believed it best to start with the "normal" and slowly transform it (which is what the great Hitchcock movies do):

> Take something normal and make it wrong. Like something like a fight between a nephew and an uncle [the inciting event in his story]. Take that—and that's not wrong—that's going to happen. That's life. Take something like that and make it go wrong. Make something that will happen, go wrong. Because that will connect people to what is really happening and it makes it scarier. Not some alien ship coming in from nowhere and blowing things up. It might be scary if you wrote it right but it is not going to be as scary as something like a dog going rabid in *Cujo*. All of a sudden you're looking at dogs and you're looking at them differently.

This was also a pattern Caroline used in her own writing:

> When you get an idea for a character—if it's going to be fantasy, just talk about their normal world, their personality, what they generally do—and then you can go into the fantasy stuff. It's better to start with the normal.

Her main character, Violet, is a dutiful daughter and student, who "sat perfectly upright at a school desk," took meticulous notes, and lived a contained life in the suburbs. But there was one source of anxiety:

> Forever there has been this strange willow tree in her back yard—and the leaves wouldn't fall off in the fall. They just turned a strange golden hue. She's always been afraid of this tree because it has something abnormal about it.

One afternoon she approaches the tree:

> Surrounding the thick trunk of the willow was a huge patch of soft, spongy moss. Treading here in her bare feet would be fun, if it wasn't for the mysterious voice whispering in Violet's head. In some places, roots as long as anacondas snaked out of the earth.

As she approaches the tree she hears a "deep and powerful female voice" warning her that without a young hero, "Malevolence will blacken the earth." After some hesitations, her quest begins.

While many students resisted structural guidelines, Jane Gilmore sees use for a conscious awareness of plot design. Gilmore runs a novel-writing program for the San Jose Area Writing Project and argues for the utility of being "literate" in the three-act plot structure, used extensively in movies, TV shows, and the stage as well as in novels (Caroline's story would map well in this structure). Once they understand it, she claims, they see it everywhere.

I asked her to lay out for me this structure, which is drawn in part from Joseph Campbell's concept of the hero's journey, and from the bible of screenwriting, Robert McKee's *Story: Substance, Structure, Style and the Principles of Screenwriting* (1997). Blake Snyder (2005) broke the three-act structure into fifteen "plot beats," which capture the progression of difficulties the protagonist faces. Jane Gilmore summarizes this progression:

> *Act 1 is about twenty percent of the novel. It is the beginning portion, the setup. It's the part of the hero's journey where he is in his ordinary world. Then there is the inciting incident (or call to adventure), the refusal of the call, and right up to the moment when the hero is going to cross the threshold into a new world or journey that's going to force growth on them.*

According to McKee, the heroes often make minimal efforts to restore their balance, but they don't work. Here is Gilmore again:

> *The first part of Act 2 is the hero acclimating to the new world; they're meeting new people, having new experiences, and they're just adjusting, learning about the world—they're not agents of their own change at this point. Act 2 is 60% of the whole novel and the hardest part to write, the hardest part to keep up the momentum. Joseph Campbell would call this the road of trials. The conflicts build on one another until you reach a midpoint where there is new information, and the protagonist is going to become an agent of their own change—they are seeking out the conflict. Act 2 ends with a climax and the resolution occurs in Act 3.*

Story, according to McKee, is all about conflict: "When conflict disappears, so do we" (211).

The continuity of plot is dependent on what McKee calls "progressions"—ever-increasing challenges for the protagonist:

> Progressions build by drawing on greater and greater capacities from characters, demanding greater and greater willpower from them, putting them at greater and greater risk, constantly passing points of no return in terms of the magnitude or quality of action. (209)

Movie classics like *On the Waterfront* build in precisely this way. And I suspect that young writers who just launch out still have some tacit awareness of this structure—it's baked in from watching *Star Wars*, *Harry Potter*, and the rest.

What Routines and Practices Help Sustain the Novel Writing?

While practices vary depending on school schedules and other demands on teachers, there do seem to be several consistent practices that make novel writing possible.

With NaNoWriMo in particular, the goal is to produce a complete draft of the novel, and the math is daunting. To produce forty thousand words in a month, you have to write thirteen hundred words each day. Students, like all writers I know, came to rely on the narcotic of word count—the gratifying daily additions to the growing manuscript. It can give rise to friendly comparisons on the playground, but more importantly, according to Grant Faulkner, it "lets them know they can do big things." Pennsylvania middle school teacher David Rockower has created an elective titled 20,000 Words; students can pick their genres and define their writing tasks, but they must hit that target.

There is a rich tradition of writers using word counts for motivation and accountability—Ernest Hemingway and Graham Greene stopping at exactly five hundred words a day (Write Only), and Stephen King (2010) clocking in at a daunting two thousand words/day.

The deadline—defined by Baty as "optimism in its most ass-kicking form" (2004, 32)—also plays a crucial role. One thing I noticed among the self-sponsored writers, who were working off the educational grid, was trouble finishing. Plots would open and open and not move toward resolution. This did not bother some writers, who just liked the process of writing. But failure to finish was frustrating for others. Knowing that you had to reach an endpoint at a certain time was a useful constraint that, it seemed to me, pushed them to control the plot.

Imagining myself in one of these classrooms, faced with this prodigious writing task, I was curious how writers could overcome blocks or times when they seem stalled. I put this question to Faulkner. Here's his response:

> *The best tool we have for writer's block is a writing sprint.*
> *We have volunteers all over the world who lead word sprints*
> *in their communities or on our Twitter account dedicated to*
> *word sprints, @NaNoWordSprints, or teachers use them in*
> *their classrooms. It's as simple as giving a prompt, a time limit*
> *of five or so minutes, and then writing as much as you can for*
> *five minutes. You can do this as an individual or in a class. I've*
> *never seen anyone not be able to write, and I've led word sprints*
> *hundreds of times. You might not use any of those words in your*
> *novel, or you might use every word. But one way or another*
> *you're exploring your idea and you're pushing it forward.*

Obviously, the word *sprint* is designed to help the writer outrun the inner censor, or inner editor, that is very likely setting a standard that is preventing writing from happening. As author and poet William Stafford advised—at such moments we have to lower our standards to a level that allows writing to happen (1990, 18).

Eighth grader Owen credited another strategy with helping him overcome a block in his novel—"writing ahead":

Owen: Believe it or not I was stuck at some points in my story—and the strategy is to write a scene well ahead of the scene you're at and then fill in the gap in between.

TN: So you know what you're pushing toward.

Owen: Exactly.

Another support mentioned by Grant Faulkner is the community support given to writers—sharing, mutual problem solving, celebrating. Eighth grader Alyssa noted that the help she got from classmates made a difference for her:

> She [Laura Bradley] helped us work with our team, and work with other people which is something I'm not used to doing. I like to be independent, and I like to work on my own. I actually got a lot of inspiration and help from my classmates which inspired some of the ideas in my book. I'm a little bit stubborn and like to do things my way, so taking someone else's opinion, modifying it and making it my own—that helped my story.

Scott Storm, a New York City teacher who builds novel writing into many of his classes, has a Novel Slam each Friday to highlight student work:

> *Friday's always a Novel Slam. The Novel Slam is just like a Poetry Slam, it's just that they're sharing their novel to the whole class. We always say you can say a sentence, tell us a paragraph. You can read a whole page. You can read a whole chapter. And the class always starts pretty timid, students thinking,* Oh I don't want to show my work to anyone I don't know. *And by week three or four it's, "Excuse me, it's my turn."*

Perhaps one of the most essential features of the novel-writing classroom: extensive (usually at least thirty minutes/class) quiet time to write.

And the advice of Alyssa bears repeating. She began, "I definitely would say work hard," but she then qualified that:

> But also don't push yourself too hard . . . You have to be in the zone to do it and you don't want to work yourself too hard so that your imagination is gone and you're writing strictly because there is a due date. You don't want to be writing because of that. You want to be writing because you're putting your heart and soul into this and you're writing about something you want to write about. You need to give yourself breaks so that you can think of something new and then you can write it down.

How Are Mentor Texts Used to Teach Fictional Skills?

In the NaNoWriMo curriculum, students are expected to choose a novel that can be used as a mentor text. I was curious about the key skills that these texts might offer as students were writing. Laura Bradley identified two—building scenes and using dialogue:

> *For a lot of students, it's the issue of not realizing how much they need to develop a scene. They'll have a scene in their head and they'll write it down almost as a summary of the scene because they haven't realized they need to take the time to show the setting and showing what the characters are thinking and doing.*

CONTROLLING NARRATIVE TIME

Clock time moves in regular increments, all seconds, minutes, hours—are exactly equal. And it moves inexorably forward. But with narrative time, writers have their fingers on the arms of the clock. A year can be described in a few sentences, and an intense minute of experience can require several paragraphs. Time can leap forward or flash backward.

To teach this key principle, fiction writer Susan Wheeler, a teacher in our writing program, developed two key exercises—time compression and time expansion—which became standards in our program.

For time compression, students choose a period of years in their lives—surviving high school, for example, or a relationship with parents, or love and breakup—and describe it in just a few sentences. I might describe my summers growing up with a series of images: spending time at Ashland, Ohio's Brookside Park—the giant company picnics, the softball games, lifeguarding on a cool summer evening, just hanging out with no place to go later in the evening.

Time expansion works the other way. It is taking an intense experience that lasted only a few minutes and writing *everything* you remember from it. Whenever I introduced this exercise, I would usually tell the story of attending the birth of our first child, Sarah. She was "turned" in the womb and required a mid-forceps delivery. The doctor had to exert such force that I was sure the baby's head would separate from the body—and her head was misshapen (temporarily) with big loop marks around the eyes—but when she did come out, she was whole and healthy. All of this I watched in a cognitive fog after "assisting" my wife in a twenty-six-hour labor.

I would also read the opening to the novel *The Trapper's Last Shot* by my colleague John Yount (1973), which opens on a hot, humid Georgia summer day: "The countryside cooked like so many vegetables in a pot." A group of boys goes to a swimming hole for relief. One of them jumps in, and instantly, dozens of water moccasins swarm around him, and fasten on to him. He barely staggers to the shore before he collapses with one snake still holding on and biting his chest.

It makes the point.

I ask students to brainstorm incidents that they remember vividly—fictionalizing if they wish—and to write everything they remember, not to censor anything. Once they come up with an incident, I encourage them to make a second list of details. (This double listing was also a standard prewriting technique).

Figure 7–1 Controlling Narrative Time

To work on scene building and other skills, Bradley continues her book shares every day and will often reproduce a page or two that shows a particular fiction-writing skill. She also creates lessons from S. E. Hinton's *The Outsiders*, which was a classroom read for all the seventh graders in the school. The best and most effective lessons, though, come from their own self-chosen mentor texts.

Here is how Elizabeth, one of her students, described how mentor texts helped her understand point of view—and decide on her own approach:

> When we started NaNoWriMo, I got super unsure of how to write dialogue, whether first or third person would be better, and when to indent. So I grabbed the two books that I had been currently reading, *Paper Towns* and *Harry Potter and the Prisoner of Azkaban*. Flipping through the first few pages, I noticed that I preferred a third-person perspective compared to first person. This is because in *Harry Potter* we could see things that Harry himself couldn't see if we were in first person. (Bradley 2018)

As Bradley notes, "Without realizing it, my students were engaging in literary analysis." One skill they turn to their mentor texts for is creating effective dialogue. The basic mechanics of punctuation and paragraphing are new to many students—they often simply go back and forth among speakers in the same paragraph. There is also the overuse of dialogue tags (. . . ," he cried painfully.). Once students get how to lay out dialogue, in my experience they often overuse it with long strings of talk that doesn't move the story forward or do anything to reveal character. Again, Bradley directs them to mentor texts:

> *One of the lessons I do with dialogue is to have them open up their own books and find dialogue, and we look at how writers do that, particularly how few tags there are, and how often the dialogue is interrupted with description and thinking.*

Another concept introduced to me by one of the students I interviewed is the "beat" popularized by Robert McKee (1997) and Blake Snyder (2005) who broke the three-act structure into fifteen beats that capture the progression of difficulties the protagonist faces.

For McKee, the *beat* (as distinguished from the much longer *plot beat*) is the smallest unit of a sequence, and we feel the flow of the scene through a progression of beats: "A *beat* is an exchange of behavior in action/reaction. Beat by beat these changing behaviors shape the running of a scene" (1997, 37). We can see this action/reaction at work in Doug's story, "The Chronicle of Old Man Jenkins." Old Man Jenkins is a character "poached" from SpongeBob SquarePants, who has been appearing in Doug's stories since first grade, literally half of his life. He has evolved into a comical superhero who, in this story, loses an arm and has it regenerated by the technical wizard Rogdai:

> "Next time that you lose an arm, there might not be a nice man with limb synthesizer all charged and ready to go. You're lucky I won't ask for coin; you seem broke enough already. Instead, I've embedded an electric chip deep in your skull," Rogdai said without remorse or consideration.

Rogdai comes across as arrogant, overly proud of his own technical skill—what does he want? Admiration, thanks, and at least some curiosity or comprehension on Jenkins' part? But he doesn't get it:

> "I don't very much like potato chips. They get stuck in my teeth," said Jenkins in his glorious stupidity.

That's a beat. Whether Jenkins is that dumb, or playing dumb, it's not what Rogdai wanted to hear, and he is aggravated.

> "No, not a potato chip you infant," said Rogdai annoyed by Jenkins. "A tracking chip but better. . . ."

Rogdai redoubles his efforts to impress Jenkins. He explains that the chips allow him to track and actually "put you and your little friends on the television, with a small bit of help from birds that aren't exactly birds." But Jenkins still plays dumb:

> "What is a—?"
> "Shut up and eat your food," Rogdai said, not willing to yield to anyone.

Another beat. He knows he is being played and ends the game. This dialogue is used effectively to show an action–reaction sequence.

How Does Grading Work?

One of the most haunting, and troubling, student interviews that I conducted was with Eva, who introduced me to the term *filters*.

> When I'm given the choice to write fiction in school it's limited or, like, filtered . . . Filtered as in—if I write something in school I know it is going to be read by someone else and I feel like that's sort of, almost like a worry that I have to make it perfect or it has to make sense to everyone else—it's a bad thing. Because if I'm writing a filtered story I know who's going to be reading it and I'm going to make sure that the words match up to what someone else would understand, whereas for me writing is intended in a certain way by the author and interpreted in as many different ways as the readers who read it.
>
> It's like seeing something that you think is beautiful—but everyone else thinks is ugly—and not caring if everyone else thinks it is ugly only that you think it is beautiful.

I asked her if teachers could be the kind of reader an author needs. Although she had had one teacher who was a good reader, she was skeptical:

> It's hard to say whether the teacher is the best person to be reading your writing because they're bringing their opinion of how creative you've been and how it fits the assignment you've been given. And there's also the comparing it to other kids in the class who are the same age and the same school. The teacher doesn't know what their life at home is like.

One of the most pernicious filters, mentioned by a number of writers (and teachers), was grading. Grading polluted the open space writers craved, it inhibited them, it shadowed them, it forced them to accommodate to an assignment or anticipate a teacher's judgment of their creativity. In short, a deal breaker. For teachers it distorted the collaborative role teachers wanted to establish. (These issues, it seems to me, apply to *all* writing instruction, not simply fiction writing.)

Can there be any more obvious premise than this: A method of evaluation should not undermine the processes it is designed to evaluate.

I was interested in how teachers—required to assign grades—navigated this responsibility in a responsible way. There seemed some consensus among teachers to avoid grading individual stories, or the novel, in the traditional comparative way that Eva found so distasteful. Since the goal is to have students engage in a set of practices that will foster individual growth, the grading system should support that.

The Tension of Grading

There are two competing, virtually incompatible, principles of assessment that pull at any teacher, including those who must grade fiction writing, or any writing for that matter. This tension keeps us up at night, or at least should. Let's call them the *quality* model and the *continuous improvement* model. The quality model is product-based and attempts to evaluate "how good" the writing is; that is its focus. It compares, ranks, sorts—rubrics help. Obviously, judgments of quality differ, but with training, readers can be brought into reasonable, though perhaps temporary, agreement.

The quality model is often more useful to institutions than to the actual writer—it helps dole out limited benefits: prizes, manuscript acceptances, admissions to programs, and often grades. It is also argued that it ensures that all students reach a uniform level of competence—providing assurance to the wider community, including future employers. But it is insensitive to the starting point of the writer, and that is its weakness when used in educational settings where students enter a class with radically different backgrounds in writing.

The continuous improvement model assumes that these differences exist. It evaluates on the basis of goals agreed on by the student and teacher. Success is not measured by achieving any uniform standard of writing quality, if such a thing exists. Rather, the focus is on engaging in processes and achieving individualized goals. This is what Don Murray meant when he coined the easily misunderstood motto "Teach the process not the product" (2009a).

It was not that he wasn't interested in good writing—but he thought the only way to get there was to have students engage in processes that writers typically engage in:

- They discover topics that engage them.
- They adopt productive writing habits.
- They learn from mentor texts.
- They set goals.
- They meet deadlines.

- They become adept at self-evaluation.
- They learn how to revise and edit.
- They become useful readers of peers' writing.

Quality is a byproduct of these writerly processes. These *habits* are the true takeaway of a writing course—and they should be the focus of a writing course, and of assessment.

The Reward of Productivity

Obviously the focus of NaNoWriMo is pushing students to write a lot in a short time—a giant first draft of a novel. Volume is a major goal; though, as Baty maintains, writers often write well *because* they are writing so much: "Writing for quantity rather than quality, I discovered, has the strange effect of bringing about both" (2004, 19). Good writing is often the byproduct of high-volume productivity, of fast, low-stress composing. Writers are evaluated on their ability to achieve their word goals—and it frankly seems inhuman to penalize in any way a student who can sustain a forty-thousand-word story for a month. That's an achievement to celebrate.

Selective Revision

Revising an entire novel would be a superhuman expectation on the part of students. But one alternative is to pick a section—maybe as few as four hundred words—and revise that section to show skill at some of the key skills in fiction writing. Here is how eighth-grade teacher Laura Bradley describes it:

> *Like all good English teachers do, you take this massive amount of writing they have done, and I say pick a two- or three-page excerpt that you revise into something you want me to assess. That's when we talk about what should be in the excerpt. I do say you need dialogue because I need to know you can write dialogue. And you need details of setting. We need to see details of character—things we've agreed throuhout the semester that a good story should have.*

It is almost as if they extract and refine a piece of micro-fiction, drawn from the novel. Other components of their grade come from shorter writing tasks used to "ramp up" and get ready to write the novel—for example, writing dialogue from a photograph or using detail to create a setting. These earlier exercises are graded.

Assessment According to Student-Generated Goals

Eighth-grade teacher Larry Graykin has created, in his own words, a "bizarre and convoluted" point system that would take the rest of this book to fully explain. But his grading of fiction writing is based on a hybrid system of student and teacher goal setting—a system sensitive to the starting point of each student. It begins with the student writing a "proposal" describing the plan, and "that gives me a chance to say, 'Gee, can you give me a little more of an idea of what you want to do here?'"

> *I have evolved a hybrid system of self-assessment and my response to their self-assessment. We use the Six Traits model of writing instruction in this school. So I have students pick a trait and I pick a trait. I like the traits because they are subjective— there is fluidity there. And I can honestly give a student a high mark if they are an emerging learner—there are elements to the rubric that I can look at and say, "Look at the success you have had" and I can give a fairly high mark, without being unfair to another student who is really working at a high school level, four or five grades above that student. I'm always looking to reinforce what's working.*

For more advanced students this hybrid assessment could borrow a standard feature of portfolio pedagogy—a commentary in which the writer self-evaluates the writing in terms of the goals or standards that are set for it, with quotations from the writing to support claims. This was a standard feature of our writing program at UNH—we often found that the commentary was the best analytic writing students did, not surprisingly because they were analyzing *themselves*, their own processes.

Fresno high school teacher Jackie Smith describes how she uses an "author's note" to assign a grade; in effect, she is not grading the "quality" of the writing, but the student's ability to engage in a decision-making process. Before the writing begins, she talks with the student about what an audience would expect:

So if students are writing a poem, they might expect interesting punctuation, they might expect a shift, they might expect a title.

In the "author's note" the student gives an account of their process in meeting these expectations:

I think about writing as a decision-making process and try to present it that way to students—as opposed to a magical process, which a lot of them think it is, or a formula. So I ask them to reflect on their decisions. Then that is what I really grade them on. So if they say, "I was going to do X and it wasn't working so I shared it with my writing group and I got these ideas and I chose this idea which I like better because. . . ." That meets my goal. That kid gets an A—because they're able to talk about their decisions.

In Don Murray's terms, this process invites "the other self"—the reflective, monitoring, metacognitive self—to speak. And it matches the earliest meaning of *assessment*, to literally "sit beside."

. . . .

One question I loved to ask was simply, "Why fiction? Why does it appeal to you?" When I asked Doug, the author of the Old Man Jenkins series, he responded:

You get to rope in so much. The human mind expands, like, inwardly forever. Like, you can make this sprawling world with this deep lore. I try to rope in all that information I have learned from across the years—the information that I read from books when I was, like, two. You've taken all this information from the outside world and you've, like, mixed and mashed it together, and you've made something that is yours. Your own world where you can dictate what happens.

Using a comparison I had heard a number of times he concluded, "It's nice to play God like that."

The sensation he and others described was a mind, supercharged, almost overwhelmed with possibilities. I think of Caroline telling me that if I could be inside her head as she planned her fiction, I would be "crushed by the flow of ideas."

It was the same story with Grayson, whose story about his autistic friend was summarized in Chapter 5:

> . . . when I write fiction my mind kind of explores different topics—connects to other movies or books or something. The ideas come together through that, like the other stuff I've read or watched before. When I start writing, my brain is this big [demonstrates with his hand] and when I keep writing it's expanding [shows] because I'm filling my brain with more vocabulary and ideas, and ways to improve my writing.

I'll end with that image: Grayson trying to convey the overwhelming fullness of his process, his hands expanding, expanding, expanding.

8

Going Close

What Does It Take to Be a
Good Reader of Student Work?

It was one of those rare smiles with a quality of eternal reassurance
in it, that you may come across four or five times in life. It faced—or
seemed to face—the whole external world for an instant, and then
concentrated on you with an irresistible prejudice in your favor.

—F. Scott Fitzgerald, *The Great Gatsby*

I'll start indirectly.

Each year I am asked to work as a judge in the Poetry Out Loud competition at our high school. Before the contest we have a brief training session
where we are given the rubric. We watch a video and assign ratings on criteria like understanding the poem, voice and intonation, and physical presence. I dutifully place numbers in each category in the practice session, and
later during the competition I do the same, hoping that I am somewhere
close to agreement with other judges.

But I am cheating.

Once the students begin their presentations, I try to get the individual criteria out of my mind—and respond to the *unitary* sensation I had from attending to their renderings of the poems. It is frankly distracting to fragment my attention and single out a feature like physical presence. Not that I feel it is unimportant—rather, all these "factors" come to me as a whole. I then quickly work my way backward to make the ratings, basically rating each individual factor the same as my overall impression.

It all reminds me of a cartoon my friend Barry Lane once created. It features Louise, broom in hand coming into her living room where her husband, Neil, poorly shaven, smoking, beer in hand, is ensconced in an easy chair watching some indeterminate show on the television. In a thought bubble Louise is pondering a rubric with ratings for "sex," "mystery," and "romance." And the caption reads, "Years later, Louise wondered if she'd used the right rubric that night she decided to marry Neil."

Of course, Barry is not suggesting a better rubric would have helped Louise—he is mocking the utility of such analytic, fragmented tools in making major decisions.

Years later, Louise wondered if she'd used the right rubric that night she decided to marry Neil.

But back to my judging, and my discomfort doing so. Those of us judging are at a table near the front of the community room at the local library—and presenters would stand not more than ten feet from us. A ninth-grade girl, nervous, would look down, take a deep breath, and begin performing her poem—and I needed to rate her on "physical presence." It felt mildly creepy. A seventy-one-year-old man judging this young girl on "physical presence." I was objectifying her, fragmenting her into aspects or features or criteria. I don't fault Poetry Out Loud for asking me to do this; it would be hard to have a contest without a rating system (and to their credit, ratings are not shared with the performer). But it crystalized why rubrics rarely work for me.

The object of the rating system was to make us more objective, less variable. But in order to be objective, that which we were judging must in some way be turned into an object. There must be a distance between observer and object—to allow for the assessment of features. My discomfort with rating the students came from objectifying them, transforming the human gesture of poetry reading into a series of features. I was turning something that was holistic and human into a thing.

The human act of response cannot be fractionalized this way. At least I can't do it. It recalls a story that former Michigan State football coach Duffy Daugherty once told after he suffered a heart attack in California following a mediocre season. He reported that he received a sympathy card from the board of trustees that read, "We wish you a fast recovery by a vote of 7–5." There are some things we shouldn't do by fractions.

In one of his most influential essays on response, Peter Elbow evaluated three forms of assessment—ranking, evaluating, and liking. He concludes that liking is the most effective form of judgment, the one most likely to build a solid relationship and help the writer. If readers have a bias toward liking they will see strengths (or potential strengths) that would be missed by someone more oriented toward criteria. The key to becoming a better writing teacher, he argues, is to become better at liking:

> How can we be better at liking? It feels as though we have no choice—as though liking and not-liking just happen to us. I don't really understand this business. I'd love to hear discussion about the mystery of liking—the phenomenology of liking. I sense it's some kind of putting oneself out—or holding oneself open—but I can't see it clearly. I have a hunch, however, that we're not so helpless about liking as we tend to feel. (1994, 14)

By foregrounding liking, Elbow shifts evaluation to the function of a relationship, not the objective assessment of traits or features. It is subjective—the reaction of one person to the gesture, the invitation, of another. While readers often like the same things (culture conditions us this way) there is an undeniably personal element in assessment.

So what makes a good reader? I believe it comes down to three attitudes.

Attentiveness

In another classic essay Donald Graves (2013b) asks the critical question—how can we avoid succumbing to orthodoxies? How do we escape the trap of routine, habit, and common wisdom? His answer was, "You pay attention to students." If you really pay attention, there's going to be something new happening that you have to respond to. And that newness is going to keep you alive.

If you just respond to the rules, or a list of features on a rubric, your field of vision will be limited. You're not likely to see anything new. The reading will be reductive, predetermined. Instead of real response we are thinking, *Is this a 3 or 4?* Even without a rubric, it is so tempting to reduce a paper to a type, just a rehash of papers you have seen before. It's a type, an imitation, not a distinctive piece of writing. We've seen it before. It instantly loses its particularity. This is a huge problem in medical diagnosis, as well—called *confirmation bias* or *anchoring* (Groopman 2007, 65): A physician decides early on what the problem is and gathers information to support that diagnosis rather than leaving the question open for a time.

But if we are attentive, fully open to the moment, to the novelty of the text, the singularity of the student—that's what's going to help us stay alive as teachers. If we can fight the urge to reduce to type or trait.

It occurred to me that if you take any student paper and copy four sentences onto Google, you will not find a match for them. Think about that. You will not find a match for those four sentences. Those four sentences have never been written before. Your reading of that paper, your connection to that student, is a unique event in human history.

There is a dramatic moment in the first act of Wagner's opera *Die Meistersinger von Nürnberg*, when aspiring singer Walther wants to join the guild of singers and has to perform a song he has composed—to be judged by the marker of the guild. Walther's free-form song, inspired by the natural world, violates all the rules of the guild (a sort of strict rubric) and the marker fills a board with symbols of his deviations. Walther is stopped before finishing. Only the shoemaker Sachs is able to respond and sings a defense. If a song departs from the rules, he argues, forget your own ways and seek out its rules. This was almost the identical advice that ninth grader Josie wanted to pass on to teachers:

Don't grade them on how their story fits into specific categories—because you don't get fiction from that, you get what you're looking for and it feels dispassionate and not really worth reading. I read some of my friends' writing, and I think this could be so good, but I know what the teacher is looking for. I know you're trying to put that in your story. Don't give anybody a rubric for fiction writing—setting, character, plot—just let them have at it and see what comes of it.

I think the same can be said for adopting a "common language" to evaluate writing—something I hear a lot. It seems to me fine to have terms like *lead*, *focus*, *voice*, and *structure*. But these cannot be used as a reductive shorthand to describe response. We need to seek out fresh language to describe what is a novel event—reading something that has never before been written. I remember one of my readers saying that in the first couple pages of an essay I seemed to be "clearing my throat"—and he was right.

Peter Elbow encourages readers to push the boundaries of metaphor in responding:

> Talk about the writing as if you were describing *voices*: for example, shouting, whining, whispering . . .
> Talk about the writing as though you were talking about *motion* or *locomotion*: for example, as marching, climbing, crawling, rolling along . . . (1973, 90)

The metaphor that works for me is magnetism. The student text is a kind of force field that exerts power over me: it may draw me in, and I feel myself literally leaning into the writing. Or it can let me go, and I feel myself no longer connected to the writing. It's physical—the body doesn't lie and it's always there first. The yawn is always an indication of something.

As I read, I pay attention to how I am attracted and released by the writing. For example, I might begin to lose attention if a quotation is too long, or if dialogue goes on too long, or if there is not enough detail for me to connect with a character. My response to the student, then, is the unpacking of reactions that are, at least initially, physical.

For me, the true image of attention will always be the great Tom Romano, who taught for many years in our summer program for teachers at the University of New Hampshire. He would hold writing conferences in the afternoon, often in the un-air-conditioned lobby of Hamilton Smith Hall. The heat would well up in the building, and by afternoon it was oppressive. Paper would stick to the skin on your arms (we once subtitled an anthology of participant writing "Writers in Heat"). And Tom would be listening to a teacher reading her writing, his concentration absolute. Nothing else mattered or interfered.

I can think of no teaching skill, no professional skill, no human skill more important (and difficult) than being present to someone else. Distraction is everywhere. We can tell when someone gives in to it—the tip-off is usually the eyes, a sideways glance. We've all been guilty of it.

We also know the gift of someone being fully present for us.

Several years ago, my wife was diagnosed with endometrial cancer, and we had a scheduled appointment with Dr. John Schorge, a gynecological oncologist working out of Massachusetts General Hospital. He patiently described what would happen, the surgery, the chemo, the hair loss, the nausea. And he asked if we had questions. I can't adequately describe the feeling of that moment, but we had the sense that time was suspended, and he had as much time as we needed as we fumbled with questions, sometimes repeated. He conveyed a calm, clarity, reassurance—that stayed with us as we went forward. He was there for us.

Curiosity

When I was directing the first-year writing program at UNH, I would sometimes just walk past the rows of offices where teachers in the program were holding conferences with students. And unobtrusively, I would make a mental tally of who was talking, teacher or student. Generally, the ratio was something like 3:1, teacher to student. There is, to be sure, no ideal ratio, and I am sure that much of the teacher talk was useful and appreciated. Students regularly claimed that the conferences were the best part of the course.

Still.

It felt like a missed opportunity, putting students in just one more position where they have to listen to an adult. I, of course, know firsthand the seductiveness of giving advice—and the way we overestimate it. It gets worse as you get older.

But all this advice giving closes off opportunities for student talk, and for learning key information about them and their composing processes. Jeff Wilhelm has coined the term *identity theme*, which I have stolen and make a central part of my teaching. An identity theme is a central interest, or an experience, or a challenge, or even a wound that shapes identity and forms an autobiographical basis for learning. It is a sort of engine—or maybe a compass. It might be surviving the divorce of parents, growing up with an autistic brother, coming from behind to win a state championship, blowing out your knee and rehabbing to return to playing D1 soccer. If I can locate these sources, I have a giant lever to use in my teaching. But to find it I have to deploy a number of writing prompts—and I have to listen.

I had good models in my parents. I grew up in a small Ohio town in the 1950s and '60s. No one had much money then and the primary form of entertainment was "dropping in" on each other, always unannounced, and sharing news, telling stories. Some of my parents' friends were great storytellers—most memorably Dick Snyder, an English professor at Ashland College, who, as I recall, played some football at the University of Indiana after the war. At one point he faced off across from a WWII vet who had lost an eye in the war, and usually had a glass eye in the socket. Except when he was playing football. Dick had to confront this cyclops. That kind of thing.

My parents were rarely the storytellers. They were the audience, and my mother was a particularly gracious listener, with the gift of drawing out these stories, and delighting in them. It was also what made her such a popular teacher. Only in retrospect did I realize that she, in particular, was as significant as the teller.

Student talk can also help teachers be effective in how we respond. In the responsive conference model that Don Murray rolled out in the second edition of *A Writer Teaches Writing* (1985), the teacher invites the writer to shape the conference. In effect the writer has an "other self" that sets goals, observes, and evaluates the writing—and in a writing conference, the teacher needs this "other self" to speak. Linda Rief, who studied with Murray, put it this way:

> *You're there as a coconspirator—"Teach me what you can teach me about this piece of writing." Tell me where you want to go*

with this, and let's see if I can help you get there. We can't know
every single nuance of who these kids are as writers and readers
unless we can sit beside them and get to their intent. I don't
know how else you can get there.

Often it is not a direct process of the student informing the teacher
of the intent—rather in the very act of talking, the student can clarify the
intent, even discover it.

One of Rief's students, Ethan, describes the way Rief's conferences
worked for him on his horror stories:

> Mrs. Rief was, like, totally helpful. She'd say, "Well, in this
> scenario, what do you think will happen next. Just say the first
> thing that will come to your mind," and she'd say, "That's weird.
> Now take it to the next level and just figure it out." And some
> teachers would be uncomfortable and be like "Oooh, what else
> could happen?" and they'd prompt you to do something else, but
> she was really supportive all the way through.

He frames this kind of reaction as a general rule:

> A teacher should be prepared to read something that they
> might not want to read—and to grade it just the same as if they
> loved it.

Ethan knew that Stephen King–like horror was not the type of fiction
that Rief—*as a private reader*—would choose to read. But she didn't see her
job as working from her personal preferences—she needed to identify, inhabit, and support the intention of the writer. Chameleonlike, teachers need
to support a range of intentions far wider than their personal reading preferences. This is an important qualification to the idea of liking—that our liking
is subsumed under the intention of the writer. We must be bigger than our
normal reading selves.

In his classic essay "The Writer's Audience Is Always a Fiction" (1975),
Walter Ong argues that an audience is not simply a collection of readers.
Rather, the writer creates a role for an audience; we are invited to be a certain
sort of reader. The reader that Ethan "invents" is one who likes to be scared,
who can suspend judgment and accept the paranormal, and sees physical

violence, and the occasional mutilation, as necessary for the genre. What Ethan is asking for is a teacher who—whatever her personal attitude toward this kind of fiction—can recognize and support the intent of the writer, who can provisionally be this kind of reader.

In my own conferences with students, I have often found it useful to articulate what I see the writer trying to do. For example, "I think you want me to see your dad as someone who makes big promises but doesn't come through." And even when I am forced to respond to a manuscript in the form of a rubric, I begin my response by summarizing what I see the writer trying to do. If I can establish my understanding and support for the "intent," a writer is more likely to see any liking as earned, and any criticism where the intent is not realized as useful and not simply a personal preference.

Jane Gilmore describes a variation of this approach, similar to another Peter Elbow (1973, 85) technique that Elbow calls "Giving Movies" of your reading—conveying to the writer your experience of reading, moment by moment. Paradoxically, this kind of response is both subjective and factual. We can't pretend that all readers would have the same experience—they won't. But there are facts in our reading—places, for example, where we are confused, or amused, or react to a character in a particular way—and it is important to convey this experience. Gilmore notes that her own practice of response has shifted toward "narrative questions":

> My rule in writing is be a reader and literally say, "As a reader
> this is what is going on in my head." One of the biggest shifts
> for me is using narrative questions. Really good writing makes
> the reader ask questions. The most common question is "What
> happens next?" But if it's good there is a very specific question
> you're asking. It's the narrative questions that carry you
> through as a reader. So I tell them what I am wondering as I
> read—and often they light up: "Oh I didn't realize that's what
> a reader could be thinking." Sometimes it will give them ideas
> for the plot, and sometimes it's like, "No, I'm off track and that's
> not what I am trying to convey."

This act of talking can also help the student (and teacher) discover what hasn't been said, what is off the page. In conferences the student can create orally an alternative or expanded text—prompted by a simple, "Tell me more about . . ." or "Why do you think . . . ?" followed by an honest silence. I have called this *the blank turn*—basically keeping my mouth shut and inviting the student to fill the silence. Maybe just giving the students a second try at saying something. In my experience, it does little good to write *expand* in the margins, when the student has not heard what could be added. Often the best part has not yet been written.

Sometimes you really get lucky.

Early in my career I was teaching a nonfiction writing course and was having a conference with a young woman who had written a lackluster paper on her hometown in Vermont. We discussed possibilities for revision, but nothing seemed to click. During a pause I noticed a Norman Rockwell postcard she had with her, and (perhaps channeling my mother) I said, "I see you have Rosie the Riveter."

"Yeah, that's my mom."

"Your mom was Rosie the Riveter???"

"Yeah," and with that she pulled out a photograph of her mother, nineteen-year-old Mary Doyle Keefe, in the Rosie pose, though not as muscular as the Rockwell version (she was a telephone operator, not a welder). It turned out that people in her town were frequent subjects for Rockwell. Spring break was near so we talked about a new paper in which she interviewed these people about what it was like to know and be painted by Rockwell.

This talk can occur, even when we have not read the student's writing— a lesson taught to me by my colleague Terry Moher. At first this felt mildly unprofessional to me—conferences should be built around reading student writing. And often that should be the case. But she showed me that the key was to have the students articulate where they were in the writing process; what, for example, was giving them difficulty. And as so often happens, when we truly name a problem, a solution, or many solutions, become evident. The conference would end with "Go try that!"

Generosity

There is a considerable debate about the role of praise in responding to student work. Alfie Kohn (2001), in particular, rejects virtually all praise as manipulative, uninstructive, and creating a sense of dependence on the teacher (e.g., "Look at how quickly Jason got in line."). And there is a virtual literature of false flattery, running from Machiavelli and Shakespeare to tales of Donald Trump.

But with writing, especially, we have to reckon with the psychological damage traditional instruction has inflicted—the bias toward negativity. Grant Faulkner, the executive director of NaNoWriMo, put it this way:

> *Students have often been taught to be alienated from writing. They're taught to not like it. They're taught to think they're not good at it, that they're deficient because they see the red marks on their papers more than they see moments of beautiful expression or eloquent persuasion. I talk to so many adults who have graduated from great colleges, who had great educations, but they don't see themselves as writers. They fear writing because somewhere within themselves they fear that they're doing it wrong.*

Papers have been marked with the ubiquitous red pen, error-focused. (Interestingly the term *rubric* shares this connection with redness, as a rubric was originally an authoritative section in a liturgical book—written in red.) In his dialogue *Phaedrus*, Plato likened a writer's fears about seeing their work disseminated to our natural anxiety about our children going into the world, unprotected.

To be sure praise can be general and sloppy. But done well it is a crucial skill for the writing teacher. Here's Peter Elbow:

> I increase the chances of my liking their writing when I get better at finding what is good—or potentially good—and learn to praise it. This is a skill. It requires a good eye, a good nose. We tend—especially in the academic world—to assume that a good eye or fine discrimination means criticizing. (1994, 14)

When we praise in this way, we do at least a few important things. We illustrate principles of good writing—we may show, for example, strong use of verbs, effective use of dialogue or descriptions—and say, in effect, "This works, do more of this."

This is exactly the kind of response that ninth grader Josie valued as she was creating a whole-novel rewrite of *The 100*.

> They [her readers] tell me the moments that they feel something. Even if they are completely loyal to the original story, and this is a deviation, they can say: "That moment I can see it, I can visualize it, I know that feels true to who they are."

She adds that they might find also an action "totally out of whack" with their understanding of the character, and Josie is open to that as well. This is a corollary that Elbow notes: We are more open to criticism if it comes from someone keenly alert to what is going right.

I also feel that it models a stance toward writing that students might internalize—a kind of self-generosity. But the predominant story we tell is that writing is painful. In fact there is a whole literature about the pain of writing—most famously this from sportswriter Red Smith: "Writing is easy. Just sit in front of a typewriter, open up a vein and bleed it out drop by drop" (Smith n.d.). I recall Don Murray saying in rebuttal, "Hell, if you find it so painful, get another line of work."

What a different image we get from the NaNoWriMo folks, with Grant Faulkner stressing the importance of "the fuel of self-belief." And Chris Baty even writing up a contract for the prospective writer in which they affirm that "I will give myself time over the next month to allow my innate gifts to come to the surface, unmolested by self-doubt, self-criticism, and other acts of self-bullying" (2004, 42).

In practice this liking can simply take the form of isolating an effective sentence or passage—and reading it aloud to the student, as literature. Sometimes that's all it takes. For novelist Pat Conroy this kind of experience was transformational. His English teacher at the Citadel, Colonel John Doyle, was an oasis of humanity in a brutal, sadistic culture. Conroy would be invited for "tea" with Doyle and his wife, and at one of these meetings, Doyle read aloud the poems Conroy had written over the summer:

> In a clear, accented voice, he read each poem aloud to me, reading them with complete openness as though they were not hopelessly amateurish and flawed. To John Doyle writing was a religious act, the teaching of it the work of holy orders. His voice lent beauty and gravitas to poems that lacked both. I couldn't

> breathe as I listened to my own words read back to me with
> uncommon gentleness. (2002, 143–44)

He would return many times to Doyle's study "to have Colonel Doyle take my writing with a seriousness it didn't deserve."

Generosity, as I imagine it, does not mean martyr-like exhaustive (and exhausting) commentary on student writing—you know, "The teacher spent more time on this paper than I did!" Such teachers exist. And they are often revered by the students who receive this intense attention—but it has always felt excessive and nonsustainable to me. As a slow reader, and slow writer, it was never even a possibility. I also believe that there is an economy to good teaching.

I've always been intrigued by the twenty-second time-out in professional basketball. It is usually called to interrupt a bad stretch, to slow the momentum of the other team. Leading up to the calling of this time-out, the coach has probably seen any number of blunders—poor shot choice, missed assignments on defense, turnovers, maybe lack of effort. He sees it all. And the coach has twenty seconds to reverse course. They can only really say one thing, make one point. What is that one thing?

Similarly, I try to prioritize. What are the one or two questions or suggestions I can make to the writer to help develop this piece of writing? I don't make a lot of marginal comments—so easy now with Word and other programs. I don't correct spelling and punctuation throughout (this takes me away from content). Often these one or two suggestions deal with the yin and yang of composing—namely, focus and material. Is it clear where the writing is going or, as Murray would quiz me, "What's this about?" And has the writer given enough detail/example/documentation at the right places? Inexperienced writers typically underestimate the detail a reader needs to feel fully present in the writing.

When I focus on the mechanics of writing, I do it in short doses. In a conference I might ask a student to pick two paragraphs, and I will go over them intensely, usually prefacing it with: "I'm going to point out everything I see in these paragraphs that can be improved."

There are well-established limits on how much information humans can take in—the bottleneck of short-term memory. In the 1950s George Miller argued that our limit is between five and nine new pieces of information (1956). It is no coincidence that some of the most influential category systems (e.g., Bloom's Taxonomy) stay within those limits. A writer can take in only so much at a time. Like the NBA coaches, I don't try to deal with everything, just take a step or two, and if we take enough of these steps we can go a long way.

Toward a Better Story of Response

It is always tricky to self-reveal as a writing teacher. There's of course that "clever" response, "I'll have to watch my grammar." But maybe worse, there is ... sympathy. "It must be tough reading all that bad writing. I hear students can't even write sentences anymore." And on and on. How self-sacrificing to be a writing teacher.

I'm thinking, *Would you say that if I said I teach basketball?* Young basketball players are equally "bad" players. They are just learning the game. They cluster around the ball, they double-dribble like crazy, they can misjudge the rim by yards. No. You would say that it is a great game, and a pleasure to help young players develop some of the skills, and that as we watch them compete, we accept the fact that they have the game only partially under control. We are generous that way, usually. And we do see skill, often in flashes, and we celebrate it. Why is writing so different? Why can't we find what Katherine Bomer (2010) calls the "hidden gems" in student writing? Why do we tell such a bad story?

It may seem that I am overemphasizing the need for positive response. For cheerleading. Isn't there a place for toughness? My response is that toughness, particularly when tinged with sarcasm or even frustration, can leave wounds that last a lifetime. When I was a first-year student at Oberlin, my European history teacher gave us an essay question that asked for a "Marxist interpretation"—I forget of what. So—writing for the first time in a bluebook, taking my first timed essay test, I wrote something on the question, completely unsure of what a Marxist interpretation was. When I picked up my graded bluebook, I saw that my grade was an F, and on this question, the teacher had written "This is more bull than knowledge." Over fifty years later, I can see that comment, see the handwriting, and relive the feeling of humiliation. It's what psychologist term a "flashbulb memory."

For a long time I thought that our anxiety about writing—the bad story we tell—was the result of this kind of punitive response. And that's part of it. But I now think it is even more basic than that—it is built into the act of writing. There is an unavoidable fear of exposure, a vulnerability that causes anxiety. How natural it is to apologize before sharing writing—to the point where some writing groups set out a bowl, and you have to drop in a quarter for any self-deprecating remark. By contrast the same group would almost never apologize about their reading skill (except maybe the reading of modern poetry). With writing, we measure ourselves (unfavorably) against published works, something readers can't really do.

We can't escape this anxiety totally, and I'm not sure that it would be good if we could. But we need to manage it. And one way to do that is, as Peter Elbow suggests, to cultivate self-generosity, to be kind to ourselves, to recognize things that work. If the only reader we can imagine is a critical one like my history teacher, we're in trouble.

We can also help to reconstruct writers' images of failure. All writing fails at certain points—but it is unproductive to have a "global" attitude toward failure. This global attitude in its extreme form is a characteristic of "learned helplessness" (Seligman 1998)—the belief that failure is nonspecific and permanent ("I'm just a bad writer"). Or it is due to a personal flaw like not trying. The antidote that we need to model is to make "failure" more technical and specific—a process that Marvin Minsky had called "depersonalizing the interior" (Bernstein 1981, 122). My humiliation in the history class came not because I was a bad student (I wasn't); there was simply a theoretical frame that I had not been taught to use—and that I could learn. A student struggling with a fictional story is not doing so because she is "just not a good fiction writer," they may need to work on dialogue in a section. It is a localized, not global, problem.

Vygotsky makes the famous claim in *Mind in Society* that we develop as humans by internalizing social patterns of interaction. The interpersonal becomes the intrapersonal (1978, 57). When we respond to student writing, there is, to be sure, the immediate help (or nonhelp) to the student. But, for better or worse, we are also providing a model of the reader that can be internalized, that can help form what Don Murray calls "the other self." If we are to create a better story about writing, we need to model a reader that can deal with our natural tendencies toward "self-bullying."

. . . .

Writing is a human gesture, an invitation—which calls for a human response, which cannot be fractionalized, reduced to a set of features. Machines can detect features, but they're not good at getting jokes or identifying with characters, or empathy. Or laughing—can there be any more undivided reaction than a good laugh? The rubrics, of course, proliferate. They are unavoidable, and I have colleagues I respect who swear by them. They get us "all on the same page." They tell students "what we want."

But I will continue to cheat.

I refuse to have my reaction parceled out in traits or features. I will try to stay whole, to view writing as a human action that invites me to be attentive, curious, and generous—to be in a relationship—helpful, I hope, but not objective, because I am attending to a human gesture and not an object.

9

Credo

What's the Story?

I'd rather write the story someone else is analyzing than
be the kid writing about someone else's story.

—Ernest

Tattoos, in my mind, are inextricably connected to the feeling of regret. You put something permanent on your skin, a saying or image or swirl of color, and what happens if, years later, your feelings about any of that changes? You're either stuck with it or have to do some painful removal.

I recall an interview with someone, heavily tattooed, who was asked about this—and the answer surprised me. She said that the tattoo was meant to be a permanent statement of value and belief, and that if, in the future, she began to reject it, she would be reminded of who she was and what she stood for. It's the same kind of thinking we use with building inscriptions: we don't worry that "Equality Under the Law" will someday become outdated. In fact, a popular website with advice for designing tattoos advises a deeply meditative first step focusing on these questions:

What are the **main themes** in your life?

What parts of your life make you **happy**?

What parts of life or yourself
are you **struggling** with?

What are your most **vivid
memories?**

What are your **goals in life?**
(Design Your Own Tattoo 2015)

What would happen then if, as English teachers, we had some tattoo that reminded us of why
we became English teachers in the first place. I
seriously doubt that we would have anything so pragmatic as "college and
career ready." That would make a miserable tattoo. It would more likely be
something about stories—telling them, reading them, and writing them.
About creativity and empathy. It would be an acknowledgment of a funda-
mental psychological principle—that our primary mode of understanding
ourselves, others, and our world is through stories. Our memory is con-
structed to retain episodes, to modify them with retellings. And it is our
primary form of pleasure as well.

Andy Molnar, a high school teacher in Los Angeles, captured the central irony of teaching high school English in the current era. He noted that
narrative and fiction writing are perceived as less rigorous than academic
argumentation and as failing to prepare students for what he called the "rig-
ors of college." The message he was receiving was that students should be
spending time framing arguments, marshalling sources, and incorporating
those sources in text citations—all skills he acknowledged should be taught.
Still.

He paused, took a breath, and continued:

> But those things are not the things that made me love writing.
> Those are not the things that we focused on in my English
> classes and made me want to be a teacher of literature. And
> I suspect that's true of everyone I've worked with. We didn't
> become English teachers so we could teach academic writing or
> argumentative writing or informational writing. The passion
> was literature and storytelling. It's funny, it's ironic that we are
> not doing more of that in our profession.

It is this disconnect that I address in this final lap of the book.

Years ago, I wrote a book with the unwieldy title *Holding On to Good Ideas in a Time of Bad Ones* (2009). No one can really remember it ("I liked your book *Hanging On . . .*"). Obviously one idea we need to hold (or hang) on to is the place of fiction writing in middle and high school. As I've noted earlier, every argument we can make for reading fiction applies even more convincingly to writing fiction. The failure to make a place for it is a tremendous missed opportunity.

My larger point is that writing has been *bound* by a set of assumptions that have limited its place and attractiveness in schools. In particular, narrative storytelling has been compartmentalized, conceived as a distinct (and often "easy") type of writing that should be handled in the lower grades. It has also been bound by its subservience to reading—which keeps it from achieving its proper place in the ELA curriculum. Time to untie these knots.

The Place of Story

Suppose I asked you this question: "Which do you want, fruit or dessert?" You would, I'd suspect, instantly recognize this as an illogical question. It might take a moment to pinpoint the problem—what philosophers would call a "category error." We have two competing principles of classification, "dessert" is a part of the meal, and "fruit" is a kind of food.

Equally problematical is the triad that is used to structure writing programs and is built into the Common Core standards—narrative, argument, and informational writing. This triad may not seem immediately illogical in the fruit/dessert sort of way, but has the same problem; namely, an inconsistent principle of classification.

Drawing on James Kinneavy's epic *A Theory of Discourse*, we need to make a distinction between the aims and modes of discourse. He defines the aims as: expressive (focusing on self); referential (focusing on informing); literary (focusing on entertainment, aesthetic pleasure); persuasive (focusing on affecting an audience's views). All aims, to some degree, are present in anything we write, but one predominates. They represent what we use language for. Modes, by contrast, represent a "principle of thought" (1971, 37). In his review of classical rhetoric he sees a consensus around four basic modes: narration, description, classification, and evaluation.

If we look at the narrative–informational–argument triad, we can see our fruit/dessert problem. "Informational" is clearly an aim; "argument" is the more logical component of the persuasive aim. But narrative is a "principle of thought," a way of understanding that underlies *all* aims. There is abundant evidence from cognitive science that we use stories as our primary means of understanding—that if I simply gave you two random words, *eggs* and *silly*, your mind would automatically begin connecting them into some kind of plot.

The triad turns into mush if we ask whether David McCullough's *John Adams* or Matthew Desmond's *Evicted*, or Malcolm Gladwell's *Outliers* are informational or narrative. They are both. As Grant Faulkner noted earlier, scientific papers have a narrative arc—they begin with some problem that needs to be resolved, some trouble, creating a kind of narrative tension. They are plotted, the reader takes a journey toward resolution. Even in the understanding of scientific information, we are deeply reliant on storytelling (Dahlstrom 2014).

It is not surprising, then, that narrative permeates all writing. As Robert McKee noted, "When conflict disappears, so do we" (1997, 221). The challenge of all writing, even writing we wouldn't normally think of as narrative, is to sustain a reading, to keep the reader moving through time. This requires the strategic insertion of narrative to anchor an idea or argument in human experience, but also an overall arc where the reader progresses from problem to resolution. Peter Elbow describes it this way:

> Successful writers lead us on a journey to satisfaction by way of expectations, frustrations, half-satisfactions, and temporary satisfactions: a well-planned sequence of yearnings and reliefs, itches and scratches. (2012, 303)

To sustain a reading, you need a plot.

To be sure, not all academic writing employs narrative as I have described, or even grounds ideas in anything visual. As readers we labor. One abstract term piles on another, and we constantly feel like we are losing our grip. To make matters worse, many academic writers seem to have an aversion to paragraphing, that magnificent invention that signals shifts in thought, and gives us a moment to catch our breath. The feeling of fatigue we quickly get when confronted with this kind of writing is biologically connected to the chemical structure for glucose that you may remember from organic chemistry (Figure 9–1).

This is what gives us quick energy. Sugar. When we are fatigued, we often have a craving for something sweet to make us more alert. According to Daniel Kahneman, this dense, narrative-averse writing requires deliberate, effortful attention—what he calls Type 2 thinking. It gradually depletes our glucose. Each sentence is work. This is not to say that we should just give up on them—but it is asking a lot of a reader to persist in a style of writing where we don't have narrative support.

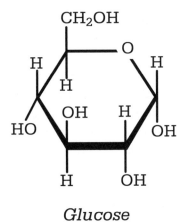

Glucose

Figure 9–1 Glucose molecule

It may seem I have wandered a good distance from any teaching implications, but I believe they are profound. It bears repeating. *Narrative is not a distinct genre of writing.* It is our primary form of understanding, hardwired in our brain. In my interview with literacy coordinator Tiffany Rehbein, she was critical of the way that the various writing types are perceived as "boxes," as distinct text types with distinct criteria and requiring distinct skills. This leads to what I have called the cattle-chute model of teaching—that to learn x (say, the research paper) you have to stay in the x chute. If you spend time, say, writing y (say, fiction) that won't help with x. And since most of the writing in the later grades shifts to informational and argument writing, time spent on fiction writing (or narrative in general) is a time-wasting diversion, maybe fun, maybe an elective for kids with tattoos, but not useful in meeting standards.

But, if narrative is seen not as a distinct text type but as our primary mode of understanding, then narrative skills underlie all the aims of discourse. Conflict is as important in argument as it is in story. And to judge from the best-sellers list, we prefer to get information through story as well. Students I interviewed, as a group, felt that fiction writing helped them with other types of writing. Grayson, for example:

> Right now [in the term after novel writing] for the magazine project we're doing expository essays, and biographies, and persuasive essays, and I feel like my brain is kind of

programmed to just write—instead of always thinking about what I'm writing. And I think fiction did that for me.

To borrow a phrase from Jackie Smith, a high school teacher I interviewed, finding a place for narrative requires teachers to "occupy a professional space." There is no escaping standards, or the curriculum of a school. But when teachers occupy a professional space, they cut through the fragmentation, reject those boxes, and leave on the shelves much of the skill-based lessons from publishers. They refuse to see their task as the hoop-jumping or exam prep. They look for the core literacy principles in those standards and reclaim agency by showing how engaging students in fiction writing, and learning from mentor texts, can teach those standards. How these practices can foster close reading, even analytic writing. And how narrative breathes life into all forms of writing.

Reading and Writing

This explosion of self-initiated fiction writing is evidence of what literacy scholar Deborah Brandt (2015) has called "the rise of writing." Increasingly we are in a writing culture shaped by legal demands for documentation, fostered by digital tools and platforms for publication that have no gatekeeping editors. Schools, in her view, have failed to keep up with this cultural shift:

> The rise of writing presents its greatest challenge to the educational enterprise, which is growing increasingly out of step with the wider world. From the start the school has defined literacy as reading and has treated writing skill as a branch of reading skill. Although recent educational initiatives have begun to emphasize more writing in the curriculum, writing remains untaught or undertaught in the nation's schools. (65)

The old equation—that we need abundant consumers (readers) but relatively few producers (writers)—simply doesn't hold. Yet in schools reading almost always trumps writing.

It may seem perverse to see writing and reading as competing forms of literacy, and it may seem reassuring to see them as parallel or complementary (Tierney and Pierson 1983). However, that is not the reality of school instruction. This bias toward reading is evident as soon as children enter school. Just listen. There is frequently "not enough time" to teach writing, but it would be irresponsible to say the same thing about reading. If there is a literacy block, writing will frequently be crowded out.

Donald Graves, in his Ford Foundation monograph "Balance the Basics: Let Them Write," was sharply critical of the almost total dominance of reading instruction in schools:

> Concern about reading is today such a political, economic, and social force in American education that an imbalance in forms of communication is guaranteed from the start of a child's schooling. The momentum of this force is such that a public reexamination of early childhood education is urgently needed. As we have seen, when writing is neglected, reading suffers. (2013a, 24)

Children are positioned to be receivers of texts, but not producers.

He also noted that teacher preparation programs failed to prepare educators to teach writing—reading methods courses were required, but writing methods courses at the time were rare and often elective. Don actually created such a course at his home institution—which, I am embarrassed to say, remains only an elective for prospective teachers.

The issue is not simply the crowding out of writing, especially fiction writing, but the subservience of writing to reading—the fact that writing is, in effect, colonized by reading. Its function is constrained to foster reading comprehension. In my day it was those irritating questions at the end of reading passages that we had to answer "in complete sentences." (Ernest mentioned how these questions diminished his reading enjoyment.) As students progress to high school, the writing that is required, especially in the higher tracks, is typically focused on literary texts.

There's a bigger problem here. Texts are not only viewed as the primary subject for writing (not food, not sports, not families, not other media, not imagined worlds)—but also students are taught to avoid the transactional experience of reading in favor of a more technical analysis. To borrow from guidelines by the creators of the Common Core ELA Standards—students are to stay within the "four corners of the text." That is, they are not to intrude feelings, judgments, reactions (that messy personal stuff)—they are to attend only to "the text itself" (Coleman and Pimentel 2011). Questions about the text, almost all of them, should be "text dependent"—they should not ask the student to engage prior knowledge or values to make judgments about characters. The text is a stable, autonomous, self-sufficient object. In other words, student readers are to bypass the very reason we read literature in the first place (Newkirk 2016).

There is a power imbalance here, a denial of the transactional nature of reading (Rosenblatt 1978); namely, the role of the reader. I see it as political. The text is authoritative and the reading process authoritarian. I use that term intentionally. In fact, the injunction to stay within the "four corners of the text" unambiguously (and probably unintentionally) introduces the metaphor of containment. The reader is contained. The role of the reader is reduced to being receptive, deferential, obedient to the demands of the text. It is consistent with conservative literalist views of the U.S. Constitution—that we should stick to what the constitution says, and not inject our interpretation. And I would say it even explains the strong appeal of phonics instruction—those letters have determinant sounds—so no guessing or predicting. The text controls the reading. It bears remembering that in George Orwell's *1984*, everyone could read—it was writing that was forbidden.

The closing off of opportunities for fiction writing in high school—and the shift to writing analyses of texts sends another political message. That there is a hierarchy with a few remote, often dead, producers of fiction—and the rest of us as consumers. If we use writing at all, it is to explicate what this higher class of authors is doing. And to make matters worse, even this analysis is often limited to features or techniques or themes—what writing *has*, not what writing *does* to the reader. Author Janet Burroway has famously said that fiction is about "trouble," characters in difficult situations, often making bad decisions—as readers we predict them, assess them, and second-guess them.

The affordances of online platforms and digital sharing make that hierarchy obsolete. Ernest said it well: "I'd rather write the story someone else is analyzing than be the kid writing about someone else's story." So writing is doubly constrained. The primary focus is on texts (writing in the service of reading), and the texts are viewed as objects to be understood and analyzed, not as actions to be responded to. I suspect there will always be diligent students who can engage with the foreshadowing in *Julius Caesar* or try to interpret the enigmatic green light in *Gatsby*. But there are literally millions who are choosing to write, off the educational grid, in free and productive spaces, creating their own worlds and characters.

Story, Time, and Memory

The great Roman essayist Seneca commented on the variable ways we recall our reading:

> There is nothing particularly surprising about the way everyone has of deriving material for their individual interests from identical subject matter. In one and the same meadow, the cow looks for grass, the dog for the hare, and the stork for the lizard. (1969, 210)

By this endpoint, I am sure you will have focused on material that speaks to your own interests and situations and forgotten a lot of the rest. You have made your own marks. So it is presumptuous of me to affirm a theme for the book, or a specific takeaway. But qualitative studies often have a particular quality that I hope my book shares. They offer as much a *way of attending* as they offer solutions or propositions or strategies. The method becomes the message. As Saul Bellow puts it at the opening to *The Adventures of Augie March*, about Augie's mother, "What I learned from her was not what she taught, but on the order of object lessons" (1953, 1).

This is the paradox of teaching (and I would say parenting as well)—that what we teach is not what is learned. Not what stays with us. We recall that history teacher, so enthralled with the Civil War that he barely made it to the twentieth century, let alone the twenty-first. Those battles blur in our mind, we can't distinguish Shiloh from Antietam. But what stays with us is the model of engagement that they imparted—what it is like to be fascinated with history.

At its best, qualitative research shows a way of listening, of attending. It is humble that way, respectful. That's the way I feel when I read my own great mentors—Shirley Heath, Anne Haas Dyson, Vivian Paley, Peter Johnston, Alfred Tatum, Luis Moll, Mike Rose, Michael Smith, Jeff Wilhelm, Deborah Brandt, and others. If I can pass on anything, I hope it is the pleasure and possibility of listening to student writers. How they opened up to a total stranger, describing their process of writing, critiquing the educational system, as well.

It was always a special moment when I would say to them: "This is going to be a weird question. But if I could go inside your head while you are writing (*pause*) what would I see?"

They would blink and then begin, "Chaos..."

And even student writing that, at first reading, did not seem exceptional was the result of a thoughtful and intriguing process. But you had to ask.

We do remember some things, some episodes in our education, vividly—for better or worse. In the opening chapter of this book I briefly, and perhaps glibly, address the concern that there simply wasn't enough time in the school day/year for fiction writing—and indeed story writing in general, or even writing in general. I want to take a last dive at this issue—and think about time, and memory, and legacy. What do we hope students retain when their time with us is over? Have we left any positive recollection, any moment? What sticks? As I have suggested, I believe that the passional style of teaching remains—but what about specifics?

The brain, after all, is set up to forget. Entire years of our schooling seem to vanish, the names of teachers slip from memory. It's a good thing that this winnowing happens, or we would be overloaded. What remains are episodes that we assemble and reassemble into a narrative of our lives. The great German poet Lisel Mueller wrote, "The story of our life / becomes our life." And we might parallel this statement with "the story of our education / becomes our education." It's not that forgotten lessons and assignments had no effect on us—but they are not *present* to us to shape our sense of self, or to be called on in times of difficulty. They've been elided from our story.

As I talked with the writers in this project, they could often remember in detail the earlier stories they wrote. Ernest could recount in mind-boggling detail the video game / story of Steve, maker of mechanical limbs. Eve recalled the spoof, "Evil Abe," that she wrote with a friend. And high school teacher Scott Storm told me the story of his high school novel writing, which involved all members of his class drawn through a portal of time—how he would read aloud to the class each new episode. These episodes are part of the educational narrative each has built.

While we can talk about scope and sequence, and an array of competencies or skills—I believe we all want to penetrate the dailiness of teaching, to create a memory, to be part of that story. I'd like to argue that by allowing for fiction writing—and narrative in general—we can do that.

A few years ago, I worked on a collection of the essays and articles of Donald Graves, whose groundbreaking work on children's writing altered the landscape of elementary education. The material included some of the videotapes we discovered in an attic at the university. These tapes dated from 1980–1982, and the "kids" on the tapes were in their early forties. But to make the tapes public, the permissions office of Heinemann insisted we track them down.

One wonderful excerpt involved a vigorous debate between two first graders. Chris Delorie had written an account of riding with his father down the Cape Cod Canal. Greg Snicer, and others in the writing group, said he should end the story with how he went back home. But Chris, pointing to the title of his story, insisted that it was about his trip and not how he got home. It went back and forth, an amazing discussion of focus.

I had heard that Chris Delorie was now a pain doctor and anesthesiologist in York, Maine. So I called his office and spoke haltingly to his receptionist: "This is going to be a weird question, but I am working on a book on children's writing and wonder if Dr. Delorie was a student at Atkinson Academy in the early 1980s." She said she thought he might be, and she promised to have him call me back.

Which he did, minutes later. He was that young writer. I was almost overcome by the compression of time—linking the six-year-old on the tape with the physician on the phone. I explained my project and asked him if he remembered the research project he was in. He said he had a vague memory of it. It was, after all, thirty-five years in the past.

Then he paused. "You know, I do remember writing about a trip with my dad down the Cape Cod Canal."

. . . .

Postscript. (April 4, 2020, 7:45 A.M.) I am recording the date and time of this writing of the last paragraphs because it is significant. Like virtually the entire country, even the majority of the world's population, I am in self-quarantine. Anxiety hovers over everything, as underprotected health workers bravely tend to the sick and dying. Deaths from the coronavirus are now a regular feature in obituaries.

Those of you reading this will, I hope, have a better sense of the outcome—and I hope that I will be there with you. But I have also found it a time of calm—even grace—as I spend time with so many activities no longer possible. I pay more attention to the birds on my front lawn, especially the robins—beautiful underappreciated birds—that are growing fat in this rainy spring. The morning is full of birdsong, most notably of the dove and cardinal.

It is also a time of reflection and self-evaluation, ironically around some of the questions that the tattoo website recommends: What are the main themes of your life? What makes you happy? Closer to the purpose of this book—what is it about teaching English that matters most to us? And can matter to our students? Not in some distant future, but now.

Sometimes it seems like we are on an endless series of deferrals, always justifying what we do in terms of some expectation in the future, which continually seems to recede and never arrives. It is never about now. The present loses its significance. Don't worry, we seem to say, that you find this tedious and dry, even formulaic—you will need it later, as if we really could predict their futures. And I suspect that skills in creativity, in visualization, and in storytelling will be part of the future, as they always have been, going back to the cave paintings of attacks on bison done twenty thousand years ago.

My worry is that we have been asked to buy a lie—or rather a series of them. That analytic writing is somehow a higher form of thinking than story; that the major function of school writing is to explicate literature; that creativity is for the talented few; that narrative is a specific text type and not our primary way of understanding; that fiction writing is unteachable and ungradable—and not really relevant for "college and career"; that rigor, not pleasure, is what we should be aiming at. If we accept these lies, we lose our birthright as English teachers.

One advantage of living with an uncertain future is that it makes you pay more attention to the present time. That may be all you have. And if we take stock of the present, of what is helping us through this time, we return to story, to the visual and specific. We watch Navy Captain Brett Crozier, cheered by his sailors, as he walks down the gangplank of his carrier after being removed from duty for warning about the outbreak of the COVID-19 virus. We are heartened by New Yorkers coming to their windows at seven each evening, banging pots and screaming thanks to health workers.

I hope that some of the great young writers I interviewed will create fiction, drawing from the horror and bravery of this time. It's as if they suddenly have a real-life dystopia on their hands. I'll close by thanking them for their generosity in talking with me—and being such articulate guides. (April 4, 2020, 8:42 A.M.)

REFERENCES

Applebee, Arthur, and Judith Langer. 2009. "What Is Happening with the Teaching of Writing." *English Journal* 98 (5): 18–25.

———. 2011. "A Snapshot of Writing Instruction in Middle Schools and High Schools." *English Journal* 110 (6): 14–27.

Atwell, Nancie. 2015. *In the Middle: A Lifetime of Learning About Writing, Reading, and Adolescents*, 3rd ed. Portsmouth, NH: Heinemann.

Atwell, Nancie, and Anne Atwell Merkel. 2016. *The Reading Zone: How to Help Kids Become Passionate, Skilled, Habitual, and Critical Readers*. New York: Scholastic.

Baker, Russell. 1982. *Growing Up*. New York: Cogdon and Weed.

Bate, W. Jackson. 1963. *John Keats*. Cambridge, MA: Harvard University Press.

Baty, Chris. 2004. *No Plot? No Problem: A Low-Stress, High-Velocity Guide to Writing a Novel in 30 Days*. San Francisco: Chronicle Books.

Bellow, Saul. 1953. *The Adventures of Augie March*. New York: Vintage.

Bernstein, Jeremy. 1981. "Profiles: Marvin Minsky's Vision of the Future." *The New Yorker* (December 14).

Bomer, Katherine. 2010. *Hidden Gems: Naming and Teaching from the Brilliance in Every Student's Writing*. Portsmouth, NH: Heinemann.

———. 2016. *The Journey Is Everything: Teaching Essays That Students Want to Write for People Who Want to Read Them*. Portsmouth, NH: Heinemann.

Bradley, Laura. 2018. "For the Love of Lit: Virtual Professional Learning Series." *PBS in the Classroom* (October 15). Available at https://www.pbs.org/education/blog/writing-with-the-great-american-read-inspiring-writers-and-engaging-readers-with-our-most-beloved-mentor-texts.

Brandt, Deborah. 2015. *The Rise of Writing: Redefining Mass Literacy.* Cambridge, UK: Cambridge University Press.

Britton, James, Tony Burgess, Nancy Martin, Alex McLeod, and Harold Rosen. 1977. *The Development of Writing Abilities (11–18).* London: Macmillan.

Burroway, Janet. n.d. "Janet Burroway Quotes." Available at https://www.azquotes.com/author/31318-Janet_Burroway.

Campbell, Joseph. 1949. *The Hero with a Thousand Faces.* Princeton, NJ: Princeton University Press.

Carr, Michelle. 2016. "Nightmares After Trauma: How Nightmares After PTSD Differ from Regular Nightmares." *Psychology Today* (March 30). Available at https://www.psychologytoday.com/us/blog/dream-factory/201603/nightmares-after-trauma.

Chiaet, Julianne. 2013. "Novel Finding: Reading Literary Fiction Improves Empathy." *Scientific American* (October 4). Available at https://www.scientificamerican.com/article/novel-finding-reading-literary-fiction-improves-empathy/.

Coleman, David. 2012. "Bringing the Common Core to Life." Video. Available at https://www.youtube.com/watch?v=Pu6lin88YXU.

Coleman, David, and Susan Pimentel. 2011. "Publishers' Criteria for the Common Core State Standards in English Language Arts and Literacy, Grades 3–12." Available at: www.corestandards.org/assets/Publishers_Criteria_for_3-12.pdf.

Collins, Suzanne. 2008. *The Hunger Games.* New York: Scholastic.

Coman, Carolyn. 1995. *What Jamie Saw.* New York: Puffin.

Conrad, Joseph. (1910) 2008. *Heart of Darkness* and *The Secret Sharer.* New York: Signet.

Conroy, Pat. 2002. *My Losing Season.* New York: Random House.

Crowley, Sharon, and Debra Hawhee. 2004. *Ancient Rhetorics for Contemporary Students.* London: Pearson.

Csikszentmihályi, Mihaly. 1990. *Flow: The Psychology of Optimal Experience.* New York: Harper & Row.

Dahlstrom, Michael F. 2014. "Using Narratives and Storytelling to Communicate Science with Nonexpert Audiences. *Proceedings of the National Academy of Sciences*. September 6 (111) (Supplement 4): 13614–20. Available at https://www.ncbi.nlm.nih.gov/pmc/articles/PMC4183170/.

Darabont, Frank, dir. 1994. *The Shawshank Redemption*. Film. Castle Rock Entertainment, released by Columbia Pictures.

Design Your Own Tattoo. n.d. www.freetattoodesigns.org/design-your-own -tattoo.html.

Desmond, Matthew. 2016. *Evicted: Poverty and Profit in the American City*. New York: Crown.

Dyson, Anne Haas. 1994. *The Social Worlds of Children Learning to Write in Urban Schools*. New York: Teachers College Press.

———. 2016. *Negotiating a Permeable Curriculum: On Literacy, Diversity, and the Interplay of Teachers' and Children's Worlds*. New York: Garn.

Elbow, Peter. 1973. *Writing Without Teachers*. New York: Oxford.

———. 1994. "Ranking, Evaluating, Liking: Sorting Out Three Forms of Judgment." *College English* 12. Retrieved from https://scholarworks.umass.edu /eng_faculty_pubs/12.

———. 2012. *Vernacular Eloquence: What Speech Can Bring to Writing*. New York: Oxford University Press.

Emig, Janet. 1983. "From the Composing Processes of 12th Graders." In *The Web of Meaning: Essays on Writing, Teaching, Learning, and Thinking*. Upper Montclair, NJ: Boynton/Cook.

Erasmus. 1963. *On Copia of Words and Ideas*. Trans. Donald B. King and H. David Rix. Milwaukee, WI: Marquette University Press.

Faulkner, Grant, Lynn Mundell, and Beret Olson, eds. 2019. *Nothing Short Of: Selected Tales from 100 Word Story*. San Francisco: Outpost19.

Ford, Richard. 2006. "How Was It to Be Dead?" *The New Yorker*, August 21. Available at https://www.newyorker.com/magazine/2006/08/28/how-was -it-to-be-dead.

Forman, Gayle. 2010. *If I Stay*. New York: Speak.

Fitzgerald, F. Scott. 2004. *The Great Gatsby*. New York: Scribner's.

Geiger, A. W., and Leslie Davis. 2019. "A Growing Number of American Teenagers—Particularly Girls—Are Facing Depression." *FactTank: News in*

Numbers (July 12). Available at https://www.pewresearch.org/fact-tank /2019/07/12/a-growing-number-of-american-teenagers-particularly-girls -are-facing-depression/.

Gere, Anne Ruggles. 1994. "Kitchen Tables and Rented Rooms: The Extracurriculum of Composition." *CCC* 45 (1): 75–92.

Giles, Gail. 2008. *What Happened to Cass McBride?* Boston: Little, Brown.

Gladwell, Malcolm. 2011. *Outliers: The Story of Success.* Boston: Little, Brown.

Golding, William. 1954. *Lord of the Flies.* London: Faber and Faber.

Graves, Donald. 2013a. "Balance the Basics: Let Them Write." In *Children Want to Write,* ed. Thomas Newkirk and Penny Kittle, 20–38. Portsmouth, NH: Heinemann.

———. 2013b. "The Enemy Is Orthodoxy." In *Children Want to Write,* ed. Thomas Newkirk and Penny Kittle, 204–15. Portsmouth, NH: Heinemann.

Green, John. 2009. *Paper Towns.* New York: Penguin.

Groopman, Jerome. 2007. *How Doctors Think.* Boston: Houghton Mifflin.

Jackson, Shirley. 1948. "The Lottery." *The New Yorker,* June 26.

James, William. 1958. *Talks to Teachers: On Psychology; and to Students on Some of Life Ideals.* New York: Norton.

Kahneman, Daniel. 2011. *Thinking, Fast and Slow.* New York: Farrar, Straus & Giroux.

King, Stephen. 1977. *The Shining.* New York: Doubleday.

———. 1981. *Cujo.* New York: Viking.

———. 1983. *Christine.* New York: Viking.

———. 1986. *It.* New York: Viking.

———. 2010. *On Writing: A Memoir of the Craft.* New York: Scribner's.

Kinneavy, James. 1971. *A Theory of Discourse.* Englewood Cliffs, NJ: Prentice-Hall.

Kohn, Alfie. 2001. "Five Reasons to Stop Saying 'Good Job.'" *Young Children* (September). Available at https://www.alfiekohn.org/article/five-reasons -stop-saying-good-job/.

Kohnen, Angela M. 2019. "Becoming a Teacher of Writing: An Analysis of Identity Resources Offered to Preservice Teachers across Contexts." *English Education* 51 (4): 348–75.

Lawrence, D. H. 2000. *The Selected Letters of D.H. Lawrence.* ed. James T. Boulton. Cambridge, UK: Cambridge University Press.

McCullough, David. 2001. *John Adams.* New York: Touchstone.

McKee, Robert. 1997. *Story: Substance, Structure, Style and the Principles of Screenwriting.* New York: HarperCollins.

Mehan, Hugh. 1979. *Learning Lessons.* Cambridge, MA: Harvard University Press.

Miller, George. 1956. "The Magical Number Seven, Plus or Minus Two: Some Limits on Our Capacity for Processing Information." *Psychological Review* 63 (2): 81–97.

Mueller, Lisel. n.d. "Why We Tell Stories." Available at https://www.poem hunter.com/best-poems/lisel-mueller/why-we-tell-stories/.

Murray, Donald. 1985. *A Writer Teaches Writing.* 2nd ed. Boston: Houghton Mifflin.

———. 1990. *Shoptalk: Learning to Write with Writers.* Portsmouth, NH: Boynton-Cook/Heinemann.

———. 2009a. "Teach Writing as a Process Not Product." In *The Essential Don Murray: Lessons from America's Greatest Writing Teacher*, ed. Thomas Newkirk and Lisa Miller, 1–5. Portsmouth, NH: Heinemann.

———. 2009b. "Teaching the Other Self: The Writer's First Reader." In *The Essential Don Murray: Lessons from America's Greatest Writing Teacher*, ed. Thomas Newkirk and Lisa Miller, 87–97. Portsmouth, NH: Heinemann.

National Novel Writing Month's Young Novelist Workbook, 5th ed. Available at https://ywp.nanowrimo.org/pages/writer-resources.

Newkirk, Thomas. 1995. "Reading People: The Pragmatic Use of Common Sense." In *When Writing Teachers Teach Literature*, ed. Art Young and Toby Fulwiler, 207–15. Portsmouth, NH: Heinemann.

———. 2002. *Misreading Masculinity: Boys, Literacy, and Popular Culture.* Portsmouth, NH: Heinemann.

———. 2009. *Holding On to Good Ideas in a Time of Bad Ones: Six Literacy Principles Worth Fighting For.* Portsmouth, NH: Heinemann.

———. 2014. *Minds Made for Stories: How We Really Read and Write Informational and Persuasive Texts.* Portsmouth, NH: Heinemann.

———. 2016. "Unbalanced Literacy: Reflections on the Common Core." *Language Arts* 93 (4): 304–11.

Ong, Walter. 1975. "The Writer's Audience Is Always a Fiction." *PMLA* 90 (1): 9–21.

Ortmeier-Hooper, Christina. 2013. *The ELL Writer: Moving Beyond Basics in the Secondary Classroom*. New York: Teachers College Press.

Paulsen, Gary. 2006. *Hatchet*. New York: Simon and Schuster.

Payne, Lucile Vaughan. 1965. *The Lively Art of Writing*. Westchester, IL: Follett.

Pearson, P. David, and Margaret Gallagher. 1983. "The Instruction of Reading Comprehension." *Contemporary Educational Psychology* 8 (3): 317–44. DOI:10.1016/0361-476X(83)90019-X.

Petersen, Wolfgang, dir. 1984. *The NeverEnding Story*. Film. Warner Brothers Pictures. Script available at https://www.imsdb.com/scripts/Neverending -Story,-The.html.

Pinker, Steven. 2014. *The Sense of Style: The Thinking Person's Guide to Writing in the 20th Century*. New York: Viking.

Plato, 2005. *Phaedrus*. Trans. Christopher Rower. London: Penguin.

Poirier, Richard. 1997. "Reading Pragmatically." In *Pragmatism: A Reader*, edited by Louis Menand, 436–55. New York: Vintage.

Radway, Janice. 1984. *Romancing the Novel: Women, Patriarchy, and Popular Culture*. Chapel Hill, NC: University of North Carolina Press.

Ray, Katie Wood. 2015. "The Journey of a Single Hour: Exploring the Rich Promise of an Immediate Release of Responsibility." In *The Teacher You Want to Be: Essays About Children, Learning, and Teaching*, ed. Matt Glover and Ellin Oliver Keene, 109–23. Portsmouth, NH: Heinemann.

Reiner, Rob, dir. 1986. *Stand by Me*. Film. Act III Productions, released by Columbia Pictures.

———. 1987. *Princess Bride*. Film. Act III Productions.

Rief, Linda. 1991. *Seeking Diversity: Language Arts with Adolescents*. Portsmouth, NH: Heinemann.

Romano, Aja. 2016. "Canon, Fanon, Shipping and More: A Glossary of the Tricky Terminology That Makes Up Fan Culture." *Vox* (June 2). Available at https://www.vox.com/2016/6/7/11858680/fandom-glossary-fanfiction-explained.

Rosenblatt, Louise. 1978. *The Reader, the Text, the Poem: The Transactional Theory of the Literary Work*. Carbondale, IL: Southern Illinois University Press.

Roth, Veronica. 2014. *Divergent*. New York: HarperCollins.

Rothenberg, Jason, creator/developer. 2014. *The 100*. TV series, 2014–2020, based on a novel series of the same name by Kass Morgan. Burbank, CA: CW Television Network.

Rowling, J. K. 1998. *Harry Potter and the Sorcerer's Stone*. New York: Scholastic.

———. 2013. *Harry Potter and the Prisoner of Azkaban*. New York: Scholastic.

Saavedra, Miguel De Cervantes. 2003. *Don Quixote*. Trans. Roberto Gonzalez Echevarria. New York: Penguin.

Salinger, J. D. 1951. *The Catcher in the Rye*. New York: Hachette.

Schacter, Daniel L. 2001. *The Seven Sins of Memory (How the Mind Forgets and Remembers)*. Boston: Houghton Mifflin Harcourt.

Schreiber, Flora Rheta. 1973. *Sybil*. New York: Warner.

Seligman, Martin. 1998. *Learned Optimism: How to Change Your Life and Your Mind*. New York: Vintage.

Seneca. 1969. *Letters from a Stoic*. New York: Penguin.

Shaughnessy, Mina. 1977. *Errors and Expectations: A Guide for the Teaching of Basic Writing*. New York: Oxford.

Shelton, Ron, dir. 1988. *Bull Durham*. The Mount Company, released by Orion Pictures. Script available at https://www.imsdb.com/scripts/Bull-Durham.html.

Smith, Red. n.d. Quote on Writing. *AZ Quotes*. Available at https://www.az-quotes.com/quote/596987.

Snyder, Blake. 2005. *Save the Cat! The Last Book on Screenwriting You'll Ever Need*. Studio City, CA: Michael Wiese Productions.

Stafford, William. 1990. "A Way of Writing." In *To Compose: Teaching Writing in High School and College*, ed. Thomas Newkirk. Portsmouth, NH: Heinemann.

Stern, Rebecca, and Grant Faulkner. 2019. *Brave the Page: A Young Writer's Guide to Telling Epic Stories*. New York: Viking.

Stern, Jerome, ed. 1996. *Micro Fiction: An Anthology of Fifty Really Short Stories*. New York: Norton.

Stevenson, Robert Louis. 2014. *The Strange Case of Dr. Jekyll and Mr. Hyde*. Open Road Media Mystery & Thriller. Available at https://openroad media.com/ebook/the-strange-case-of-dr-jekyll-and-mr-hyde /9781480484146.

Strout, Elizabeth. 2019. "Motherless Child." *New Yorker*, August 5. Available at https://www.newyorker.com/magazine/2019/08/05/motherless-child.

Suskind, Ron. 2014. "Reaching My Son Through Disney." *New York Times Magazine*, March 7. Available at https://www.nytimes.com/2014/03/09 /magazine/reaching-my-autistic-son-through-disney.html.

Teaching Secondary Students to Write Effectively. 2017. Washington, DC: Institute of Educational Sciences, U.S. Department of Education. Available at https://ies.ed.gov/ncee/wwc/Docs/PracticeGuide/wwc_secondary _writing_110116.pdf.

Tierney, Robert, and David Pearson. 1983. "Toward a Composing Model of Reading." *Language Arts* 60 (5): 568–80.

Tisch, Steve. 2018. "Arthur Miller Failed a Profound Moral Test. What Should We Now Think of His Plays?" *USA Today* (June 25). Available at https:// www.usatoday.com/story/opinion/2018/06/25/arthur-millers-down -syndrome-son-tarnishes-moral-artistic-legacy-column/725003002/.

Twain, Mark. 1885. *The Adventures of Huckleberry Finn*. A Glassbook Classic. Available at https://contentserver.adobe.com/store/books/HuckFinn.pdf.

Vidali, Amy. 2007. "Performing the Rhetorical Freak Show: Disability, Student Writing, and College Admissions." *College English* 69 (6): 615–41.

Vygotsky, L. S. 1978. *Mind in Society: The Development of Higher Psychological Processes*. Ed. Michael Cole, Vera John-Steiner, Sylvia Scribner, and Ellen Souberman. Cambridge, MA: Harvard University Press.

Wagner, Richard. 2015. *Die Meistersinger von Nürnberg*. Libretto trans. Peter Branscombe. London, UK: Overture.

Warner, John. 2019. *The Writers Practice: Building Confidence in Your Nonfiction Writing*. New York: Penguin.

Wight, Shauna. 2017. "Admitted or Denied: Multilingual Writers Negotiate Admissions Essays." *Journal of Adolescent and Adult Literacy* 61 (2): 141–51.

Wilhelm, Jeffrey. 1997. *"You Gotta Be the Book": Teaching Engaged and Reflective Reading with Adolescents*. New York: Teachers College Press.

Wilhelm, Jeffrey, Michael W. Smith, and Sharon Fransen. 2014. *Reading Unbound: Why Kids Need to Read What They Want—And Why We Should Let Them*. New York: Scholastic.

"Write Only 500 Words Per Day and Publish 50+ Books: Graham Greene's Writing Method." *Open Culture*. Available at http://www.openculture.com

/2020/05/write-only-500-words-per-day-and-publish-50-books-graham
-greenes-writing-method.html.

Yalom, Irvin D. 2012. *Love's Executioner: And Other Tales of Psychotherapy.*
Boston: Basic Books.

Yount, John. 1973. *The Trapper's Last Shot.* New York: Random House.

Zemeckis, Robert, dir. 1985. *Back to the Future.* Film. Universal City, CA:
Universal Pictures. Script available at http://www.dailyscript.com/scripts
/bttf4th.pdf.